# How to Feed Your Whole Family a Healthy, Balanced Diet

# How to Feed Your Whole Family a Healthy, Balanced Diet

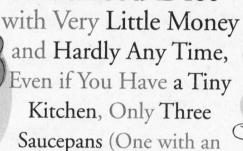

with Very Little Money and Hardly Any Time, Even if You Have a Tiny Kitchen, Only Three Saucepans (One with an Ill-Fitting Lid), and No Fancy Gadgets—Unless You Count the Garlic Crusher . . .

**Simple, wholesome, and nutritious recipes for family meals**

## GILL HOLCOMBE

St. Martin's Griffin
New York

# Acknowledgments

I'd like to thank the following people for passing on tips and recipes and sharing their knowledge and expertise. They are: Jean Hack, Barbara Holcombe, Irene Rutman, Doreen Gould, June Greenland, Daphne Croucher, and Norah Pearce; also Tim Hack, Claire Orencas, Carole Moore, and Sarah Todd. And last but not least I'd like to thank my three children, Oliver, Billy, and Eleanor, who eat everything up and make it all worthwhile.

# Contents

INTRODUCTION / 1
Getting Started / 5
A Word About Weight Loss / 7
Basic Store Pantry Ingredients / 9
Herbs & Spices / 10
Preparing Vegetables / 12
Notes / 14

I WAKE UP TO BREAKFAST /
    17
Everyday breakfasts / 18
Weekend breakfasts / 24

2 LITTLE GEMS AND TOUGH
    COOKIES / 27
Fussy Eaters / 28
Packed Lunches / 32

3 MAKE DINNER, NOT EXCUSES /
    39
Main recipes:
Shepherd's Pie / 40
Moussaka / 42
Chili Con Carne / 43
Hamburgers / 45
Rissoles / 46
Chicken Nuggets / 48
Chicken Curry / 50
Mexican Chicken / 51
Chicken & Ham Pasta Bake / 52
Sweet & Sour Chicken / 54
Toad in the Hole / 56

Cider Sauce for Sausages / 57
Sausage Rolls / 59
Sweet Apple & Apricot Pork / 61
Ginger Beer Pork / 62
Spicy Pork Meatballs / 62
Beef Stroganoff / 64
Lancashire Hot Pot / 65
Chicken Liver Risotto / 68
Tuna Lasagne / 71
Sweet & Spicy Shrimp / 72
Kedgeree / 73
Fish Cakes / 75
Stuffed Peppers / 77
Stuffed Mushrooms / 78
Veggie Burgers / 79
Eggplant Lasagne / 80
Lentil Moussaka / 82
Rice Salad / 84
Nut-free Nut Roast / 86
Pizza / 87
Baked Potato Pizzas / 90
Cheese & Onion Tomatoes / 91
DIY Pasta Sauce / 93
Ratatouille / 95

Recipes in brief:
Beef & Cheese Crumble / 47
Chicken in Cream & Mushroom
    Sauce / 55
Chicken Goujons / 55
Jamie Oliver–Style Pan-Fried Sausages / 58
Sausages in Curry Sauce / 58
Pork in Plum Sauce / 63

# Contents

Greek-style Pork / 63
Beef Curry / 65
Kebabs / 66
Medallions of Lamb in Red Wine / 67
Liver in Black Bean Sauce / 69
Mixed Grill / 70
Spicy Liver & Pork Meatballs / 70
Fish Pie / 76
Broiled Sardines / 76

4 QUICK FIXES / 99
Pacific Pie / 100
Noodles / 101
More Noodles / 102
Bacon Cakes / 103
One-Step Pasta / 104
Instant Corned Beef Hash / 104
Shrimp & Egg Pie / 105
Fish Stick Pie / 106
Smoked Salmon Tagliatelle / 107
Fastest-ever Fishcakes / 108
Things on Toast / 109

5 THE JOY OF SOUP / 111
Orange Squash / 112
Celery / 113
Watercress / 114
Stinging Nettle / 115
Sweet Potato / 116
Lentil & Vegetable / 117
Spicy Bean / 118
Tomato & Red Lentil / 119
Minestrone / 120
Smoked Mackerel Chowder / 122
Borsht / 123
Chicken / 124

Scotch Broth / 126
Cool Cucumber / 128
Hot or Cold Leek & Potato / 129

6 JOIN THE PUDDING CLUB / 133
Main recipes:
Cherry Cheesecake / 135
Lemon Cheesecake / 137
Cheshire Tart / 138
Baked Apples / 139
Rhubarb Crumble / 141
Poor Man's Apple Pie / 142
Banana-Orange Trifle / 142
Bread & Butter Pudding / 143
Raspberry Ice-Cream / 144
Chocolate Mousse / 146
Treacle Tart / 147
Tiramisu / 148
Fruit Fool / 149
Spotted Dick / 150

Recipes in brief:
Strawberry Meringues / 151
Orange Cups / 151
Baked Banana Custard / 152
Fruit Jell-O / 152

7 CANT COOK? DONT COOK! / 155
Smoothies / 156
Isotonic Drinks / 157

8 LET THEM EAT CAKE / 159
Cooking with children:
Easy Cheesy Shortbreads / 165
Cheese & Zucchini Scones / 166
Jam Tarts / 167

*Chocolate Rice Krispies Cakes* / 168
*Cornflake Cakes* / 169
*Cup Cakes* / 169
*Gingerbread Men* / 171
*Sweetloaf* / 172
*Treacle Crunches* / 174
*Chocolate Chip Cookies* / 175

Wholesome cakes:
*Carrot Cake* / 176
*Bran Loaf* / 177
*Rock Cakes* / 178
*Ginger Cake* / 179
*Banana Cake* / 181
*All-in-One Apple Cake* / 182
*Bread Pudding* / 183
*Flapjacks* / 183
*Seed Cake* / 184
*Plum Cake* / 186
*Almond & Apricot Muffins* / 187
*Muesli Muffins* / 188
*Pumpkin Muffins* / 189

Special cakes:
*Jelly Roll* / 190
*Caterpillar Cake* / 193
*Chocolate Yule Log* / 194
*Layer Cake* / 195
*Honey, Lemon & Yogurt Cake* / 196
*The Ultimate Chocolate Cake* / 197
*Chocolate Caramel Cakes* / 199

9 NOT ONLY BUT ALSO / 203
*Quick Brown Bread* / 203
*Soda Bread* / 204
*Garlic Bread* / 206

*Guacamole* / 207
*Hummus* / 207
*Roasted Nuts* / 208
*Mayonnaise* / 209
*Potato Salad* / 210
*Hash Browns* / 210
*Hot Cross Buns* / 211
*Honeycomb* / 214
*Ginger Beer* / 215
*Toffee Apples* / 217
*Chutney* / 218
*Soft Fruit Spread* / 220
*Grapefruit Curd* / 221
*Figgy Pudding* / 222
*Fudge* / 224

10 WEEKLY MENU PLANNING / 229
*Chili Con Carne & Rice* / 233
*Chili & Chips* / 234
*Veggie Burgers & Potato Wedges* / 234
*Chinese Chicken Stir-Fry* / 235
*Frankfurters & DIY Pasta Sauce* / 235
*Roast Chicken* / 236
*Chicken & Leek Casserole* / 237
*Bubble, Bangers & Beans* / 238
*Kedgeree* / 239
*Cheese & Spinach Omelette* / 239
*Boiled Bacon & Roasted Vegetables* / 241
*Vegetable Tortilla* / 243
*Pork Meatballs, Tagliatelli & Tomato Sauce* / 244
*Stuffed Peppers* / 244
*Pacific Pie* / 245

*Liver, Bacon & Onions* / 246
*Tomato & Red Lentil Soup* / 247
*Salmon & Tomato Pasta Bake* / 247
*Pork Loin Steaks, Sausages & Rice* /
    248
*Bread Roll Pizzas* / 249
*Corned Beef Hash* / 250

*Fish Stick Pie* / 251
*Spaghetti Bolognese* / 251
*Curried Nut Roast* / 252
*Ham Steaks, Egg & Homemade*
    *Fries* / 253

*Index* / 256

# Introduction

*Have you ever spent a small fortune in the supermarket and still struggled to put a decent meal together? Are your children always complaining they're hungry even though they eat constantly? Do you own a set of expensive saucepans or have a kitchen full of gadgets you never use? Would you like to cook more and eat together as a family if only you had the time?*

Time, or lack of it, is probably the reason most of us give for not cooking these days, but less than forty years ago almost everyone cooked at least one proper meal from scratch every day even though not everyone owned a fridge, let alone all the other labor-saving devices we take for granted today. Maybe we do have more commitments in some areas of our lives than previous generations, but when it comes to food, not only do we have a much greater variety to choose from, we also have twenty-four-hour supermarkets, Internet shopping, home deliveries, endless cooking programs on TV, hundreds of cookbooks, and microwave ovens that sell for smaller sums of money than you'd spend on a family meal in a fast-food outlet.

To hear some people talk you'd think no one had ever been busy until about 1985, but no matter where you live or what your circumstances are, the truth is it's still possible to put a balanced meal together in less time that it takes to order in a pizza and wait for it to be delivered (cold usually) to your door.

And if recent reports are to be believed, there must be more cookbooks gathering dust in designer kitchens in this country than there are people who cook regularly, so apart from the old argument about having no time, what's putting people off?

It's easy to be taken in by some convenience foods; beautifully packaged, cleverly advertised, and presented as healthy food that's good for us and will make life easier. But what thousands of people probably don't realize is that they can make a far better shepherd's pie or toad in the hole themselves just by following a very simple recipe—and who can blame them? So seductive are some of the TV commercials, you could be forgiven for thinking it's a privilege to be allowed inside the shop to spend your money in the first place.

But no one's doing us any favors, least of all the major stores with their gorgeous displays, catchy slogans, and buy-one-get-one-free deals. And even though the ingredients in every product are printed on the packaging it's easy to be misled. People in a hurry tend to grab whatever looks good and place their trust in the brand name without stopping to study the small print, or even really knowing what they're looking for.

The funny thing about convenience food is it's not even that convenient. Once you've removed the packaging, read the instructions, pierced the plastic film (or not), waited, taken the tray out halfway through the cooking time to stir the food, waited again, let it stand for two minutes, scalded yourself on the steam, searched in vain for a piece of meat among the gunk, wolfed the lot in four minutes flat, and wondered what else there is to eat because you're still hungry, it might occur to you that the little bit of effort you saved by not cooking your own dinner wasn't really justified by the end result.

The other food myth that often gets repeated is that the unhealthiest foods are the least expensive, and that some people, especially families on very low incomes, only resort to eating them because they have no choice. But this simply isn't true. A week's worth of good-quality meat and fish with lots of potatoes, rice, pasta, vegetables, fruit, and other whole foods costs no more than the same amount of cheap chicken, burgers, pies, reconstituted potatoes, instant microwave meals, and carbonated drinks.

I know cooking isn't everyone's idea of fun and some people will never enjoy it, which is why this book isn't about learning to cook complicated meals that take hours to prepare and only minutes for your kids to reject. You don't have to be a great cook, or even a particularly good one. You don't have to go shopping more often than you want to, or spend more money than you can afford. There's nothing here that you can't buy from any of the big supermarkets—assuming that's where you do your shopping because, like me, you're not lucky enough to have anything better where you live. Some of the recipes can be thrown together in minutes and a very few don't involve any cooking at all. True, they all contain a certain amount of fat, sugar, and salt, but nowhere near as much as you'd find in commercially prepared food—and at least the nutrients are there as well.

There seems to be an ever-changing list of so-called super foods these days and I even came across a series of articles in one parenting magazine under what I thought was the very bad taste headline: "Cancer-proof Your Kids." But in spite of so much food knowledge there are still people who think we need sugar for energy (not necessarily; we get energy from all our food), that diet colas are better than those containing sugar when they're potentially worse (because of the chemicals in artificial sweeteners), or who, when asked to name a typical English food, say "quiche."

I read recently that thousands of primary school children don't know where eggs come from, or which meat comes from which animal, and that's not surprising if it's also true—as yet another survey claimed—that a fifth of adults don't know where sausages and bacon come from, or what the main ingredient of yogurt is. And it's strange that we can be so squeamish about fresh raw meat and organ meats when we happily eat far more unsavoury bits of the animal (eyeballs, genitals, you name it) in burgers, kebabs, and sausages.

When I was a child growing up in the 1970s, a healthy meal was meat and three veggies followed by a fruit dessert. Takeout meant the occasional trip to the fish and chip shop, and for something continental there was an occasional curry. Now we can laugh, but people worried a lot less about food in those days, no one obsessed about their five portions a day; far more people stayed effortlessly slim, women apparently had smaller waistlines, obesity and obesity-related diseases were a lot less common, and a seriously overweight child was rarer than a white Christmas.

Much has been made in the past about the history of our unhealthy British diet, but it doesn't seem to me to have been too bad for what was, traditionally, a skinny population inhabiting a chilly little island off the North Sea. We may have had something to learn about the way we cooked our vegetables (like how to steam instead of boiling them to death) but what's wrong with potatoes, puddings, and pies, as long as you're eating your greens? To my way of thinking a proper home-cooked meal—with or without fries—is worth a dozen fast-food hits that leave you with nothing but a craving for something sweet and a raging thirst.

Miracle foods come and go, but whether the current flavor of the month is wheatgrass, alfalfa sprouts, or Goji berries, the secret of feeding good food to your family without chaining yourself to the kitchen, depriving your children of the things they like to eat, and driving yourself round the bend is that really, there is no secret. The answer was here all along.

# GETTING STARTED

*Whenever I come across a recipe containing mace (a spice made from the husk of a nutmeg), a liqueur, or some other exotic, hard-to-get-hold-of ingredient I know I'll never use again, I immediately lose interest.*

One of my friends says she's put off by arty photographs of vegetables tied up in little parcels and anything else that looks too fiddly and refined, and to those two objections I would add recipes with too many ingredients, or too many stages from start to finish; something with a long preparation *and* a long cooking time (one or the other is just about okay), anything that requires a piece of equipment I don't have and may not have heard of, and anything that uses lots of pots and pans and makes too much washing up. I've also got an irrational fear of recipes containing gelatin, a perfectly rational fear of soufflés, and until quite recently I'd steer clear of lentils if they had to be soaked overnight. Why, I don't know, since putting lentils in a bowl of cold water and rinsing them in a sieve takes about the same amount of time and energy as making a cup of tea, and I do that all the time.

It's all very well for celebrity chefs to say they want to get women back into the kitchen. What they don't seem to realize is that many people, myself included, owning nothing more sophisticated than a four-sided cheese grater, feel ruthlessly excluded by references to blini pans, griddles, and pasta-making machines before we even start.

Having said that, if you're serious about improving your family's eating habits, there are a few pieces of equipment you can't afford to be without, and in homes that have wide-screen TV, DVDs, iPods, and game consoles in every room, none of them is exactly hi-tech. An electric hand mixer is perfect for making cakes, among other things, while a food processor or blender (preferably 2 quarts plus) is good for mixing, beating, and blending large quantities of anything and everything. The price of electrical goods is always coming down, so you shouldn't have any trouble finding these things for sale at around five pounds for a hand whisk and twenty pounds for a food processor. On the manual side, all the mixing bowls, casserole dishes, saucepans, cake pans, whisks, spoons, and any other bits and pieces you need can be bought dirt cheap from the local supermarket or discount store.

If you already have the right equipment and it's lack of confidence more than anything that keeps you from being more adventurous in the kitchen, stop worrying. It's practically unheard of for anyone to poison their family (by accident) and you're unlikely to experience worse disasters than a burned saucepan or food that's a bit browner around the edges than it was meant to be. Learning to cook is a bit like learning to drive. It only looks difficult from the outside. Once you realize you're the one in control of the machinery and not the other way around there's nothing to it.

Don't worry about spending too many lonely hours in the kitchen on your own either. For one thing, there's nothing to stop you listening to the radio or having the television on if you need company. You can also drink alcohol and use your cell phone while operating a food processor without breaking the law. It's even better if you can get the kids to help, which doesn't mean you have to let them waste your valuable time and make a mess of the kitchen while you grit your teeth and smile indulgently like an imaginary, perfect mother in a TV commercial. What you need is an assistant; someone to get the stuff out of the fridge for you, fetch whatever you need, open the packages, put the vegetable peelings in the right trash can (careful now), help with the tidying up, and stir whatever you're cooking while you save all the best jobs for yourself. Not only is it possible to cut the preparation time right down, the children are picking up a set of good practical skills in the process without even realizing you're teaching them a lesson. How perfect is that?

No matter how good your intentions are there are bound to be times when it all goes pear-shaped and you find yourself eating crackers and cheese for dinner three nights in a row, but there's always a solution to the eternal time problem regardless of whether you're a stay-at-home parent or working—or a bit of both. It's just a case of finding out what works best for you. My advice is to cook more and do less ironing (or none at all) and think about what you're going to eat when you *do* have a bit of time, whenever that may be . . .

Some people say we've lost a whole generation, if not two, to the fast-food culture and there's little hope of things changing for the better in the future, but I'm more optimistic than that. For one thing the social and economic advantages of cooking and eating at home speak for themselves. Not twenty years ago people were predicting we'd be getting all our reading material from the Internet by now and that books would be obsolete, but there's no sign of that happening any time soon.

With one health scare after another (Mad Cow Disease, foot and mouth, GM foods) and so much evidence pointing to the ill-effects a terrible diet is having on our children, it can only be a matter of time before the tide turns back in favor of preparing and cooking our own food once and for all.

## A WORD ABOUT WEIGHT LOSS

*This is a recipe book not a diet book, but if you switch from commercially prepared and processed food to mostly healthy ingredients and stop fretting about what you can and can't eat, you and your family are bound to lose weight, look better, feel fitter, have more energy—and be happier.*

Apart from stuffing yourself with poor-quality food, nothing is more likely to make you put on weight than constant, miserable, half-hearted attempts to stop eating the things you like.

I don't think it's worth torturing yourself by trying to resist the odd craving for something "unhealthy" whether it's fast food, drinks, or sweets. But realistically, genuine cravings don't happen every day (unless you're pregnant), and nobody puts on weight by eating a chocolate bar and a takeout meal once a week. To pile on the pounds you have to be eating chronically badly practically all the time.

When you stop and think about how you feel two hours after a fast-food meal (hungry, thirsty, and desperate for something sweet) compared with how you feel when you've eaten something truly nutritious, the advantages of good food over junk should be obvious. In fact, I don't know why we expect to have to suffer to be healthy when the opposite is true.

On the subject of bad eating habits, it's impossible to ignore what must be the most pointless and easily avoidable evil of them all: carbonated drinks.

Never mind chocolate, fries, and bacon sandwiches. Even a burger with bright orange cheese and rubbery bits of gherkin has a certain appeal at times. But what's with the carbonated water? I don't get it. Carbonated drinks are either pretty bland or sickly sweet; too gassy, full of sugar or artificial sweeteners, and not only do they *not* do what they're supposed to, they actually make you thirstier than you were to start with, so you have to drink even more. It's brilliant! For the manufacturers, it's brilliant. Not so great for you, your weight, your teeth, and your general health. Yet countless thousands or, God forbid, millions of people still drink this stuff every single day. And from what I've seen and heard, some people hardly drink anything else. Why?

# BASIC PANTRY INGREDIENTS

*The same ingredients crop up time and time again in these recipes. Keeping lots of nonperishable items in the pantry makes life easier and means never having to say you're sorry, but it's cornflakes for dinner again tonight . . .*

The ingredients listed below have a long shelf life, and as well as having a huge number of uses they're also very affordable, so stock up on as many of these items as you can and you'll always have something to make a meal out of.

## CANS
FISH (sardines, pilchards, salmon, tuna)
VEGETABLES (chopped tomatoes, plum tomatoes, corn kernels, imported British mushy peas, mixed)
FRUIT (peaches, pears, pineapple, mixed)
BEANS (baked, borlotti, cannellini, butter beans, broad beans, mixed)
CORNED BEEF

## DRIED
FRUIT (apricots, prunes, dark and golden raisins, cranberries, mixed)
LENTILS AND PULSES (red lentils, green lentils, mung beans, yellow split peas, chickpeas)
RICE (brown, basmati)
NUTS (peanuts, cashews, almonds, mixed)
SEEDS (sesame, pumpkin, sunflower, mixed)
FLOUR (all-purpose, self-raising, whole wheat, bread flour)
SUGAR (superfine granulated, regular granulated, and light brown)

ALSO pasta, oatmeal, couscous, soup mix, salt, pepper, herbs, and spices.

## BOTTLES
OIL (vegetable or corn oil, olive oil, sesame oil)
VINEGAR (malt, cider, balsamic)
ALSO lemon juice, lime juice, Worcestershire sauce, soy sauce, sherry, and golden and maple syrup.

## OTHER
PUREES (tomato paste, garlic paste, red and green pesto)
MUSTARD (English, French, Dijon)
ALSO stock cubes, instant gravy granules, Marmite or Vegemite.

———

Note: *And one more thing I couldn't live without*—plain to live-culture yogurt. It has 101 uses in curries, soups, sauces, cakes, and smoothies, as well as being perfect with fruit, nuts, and honey, or simply on its own. One helping is all you need to get the right balance of probiotics, without wasting money on fashionable, fruit flavored "healthy" yogurt drinks.

# HERBS AND SPICES

———

*What on earth did we do before the use of herbs and spices in everyday cooking finally caught on in the average household sometime in the seventies?*

———

Until then lots of families had never experienced anything more exotic than mint sauce with roast lamb or mixed spices in home-made fruitcake. Now most people have herbs and spices at home, but some people still aren't using them, which is a pity. Herbs and spices add tremendous depth and flavor to all kinds of sweet and savory food, and nobody—whether you're wildly enthusiastic about cooking, or a bit on the lazy side like me—should be without them. (Every supermarket should have a good selection.)

Tomato ketchup has its uses, but smother your dinner in tomato ketchup and all it tastes of is tomato ketchup, whereas herbs and spices complement and enhance the flavor of the food itself, without necessarily making it too strong and spicy. When you're used to eating food that actually tastes of something you don't feel the need for a chemical-laden, fast-food hit anywhere near as often as you do when your diet consists mainly of processed junk.

Fresh herbs can also be bought in the supermarket, although the range tends to be more limited, but if you want to use fresh instead of dried herbs in any of these recipes, that's even better.

Advice about which herbs and spices go well with certain foods is nearly always printed on the packaging you buy them in, but for the record, here are a few of the most popular and versatile ones, and a general idea of how to use them.

GINGER Warm and spicy, especially good with lemon and lime juice, and brown sugar in stir-fries, curries, cakes, cookies, drinks, and soup—you name it.

CURRY POWDER/CHILI POWDER Usually sold in mild, medium, and hot, I tend to buy hot because, rightly or wrongly, I can't help feeling I must be getting more spice for my money that way. If I want less heat I just use less spice.

CUMIN, GROUND/CUMIN SEEDS Boosts the effect of curry and chili powder and add their own flavor.

CORIANDER, GROUND Great in curries, Mexican dishes, and in carrot, and other orange vegetable soups.

PARSLEY Sprinkle over tomato, potato, egg, cheese, and fish dishes.

CHIVES Omelettes, potato salad, vegetable dishes.

ROSEMARY Great with roast lamb, shepherd's pie, some chicken dishes; also good with roast potatoes.

SAGE Great with pork, sausages, and onions; also homemade stuffing.

TARRAGON Some fish and most chicken dishes (also good mixed with the bread-crumb coating on chicken goujons).

PAPRIKA Subtly different from CAYENNE PEPPER, which is more fiery where paprika is milder and sweeter. Use paprika for a subtle flavor and cayenne pepper when you want more heat.

MIXED HERBS A good all round substitute when you've run out of everything else.

PUMPKIN PIE OR APPLE PIE SPICE MIX Good in cakes and cookies, and as an alternative to ALLSPICE, which is similar but sharper; tasting more heavily of cloves. Use in savory dishes as well; stir-fries, for example.

CINNAMON, GROUND Sweet and spicy, perfect with apples in cakes, desserts, and cookies.

NUTMEG, GROUND Good with spinach—especially where spinach is one of the main ingredients—and perfect in spicy fruit-cakes, cookies, and banana smoothies.

## PREPARING VEGETABLES

*I didn't know what to do with fennel before Jamie Oliver came along, so just in case, here's everything you wanted to know about preparing and cooking vegetables but were afraid to ask . . .*

ARTICHOKES Remove the stalk and the tough or damaged outer leaves, then wash well, slice into quarters lengthwise, and get rid of the hairy center bit, or choke. *To cook:* In fact, there are no recipes containing artichokes in this book, but if that wasn't enough to put you off and you feel like adding artichokes to soup, stews, or casseroles, good luck to you.

ASPARAGUS Cut off the tough ends to make all the asparagus spears the same length (although the supermarket may have already done this) and wash in cold water. *To cook*: Simmer gently in boiling water for 5–10 minutes, or place in a casserole dish with a lid, cover with a little cold water, and cook in the microwave for 3–4 minutes.

EGGPLANT Cut off the stem end and bottom end and discard. Cut crosswise into thin slices and soak in a bowl of salty water for about 10 minutes, then strain away the brown, salty water and dry with paper towels, or an old, clean tea towel. *To cook*: Deep-fry the slices in very hot oil (about 3 inches [6cm] deep will do, you don't need to fill the whole pan) as quickly as you can to stop them soaking up too much oil. For a healthier alternative, eggplant slices can be brushed with olive oil and baked.

BEETS Remove the long root and leave a bit of the stems, wash, and cut into quarters, but don't bother to peel. *To cook*: Bring to the boil in cold water and simmer gently for a good half an hour, then the skin can easily be rubbed off. The beets can be eaten at this stage, or drizzled with olive oil and roasted in the oven.

BUTTERNUT SQUASH Wash and cut about ½ inch (2cm) off either end. Cut in half lengthwise; scrape out the spongy inner bit, and remove the seeds. Peel each half with a potato peeler or sharp knife (the skin is very tough) then cut into chunks. Alternatively, cut into chunks and cook the squash *first*, removing the skin after cooking when the squash is much softer. *To cook*: Boil and then mash with butter and milk (starting in cold water, as with boiled potatoes), or drizzle with olive oil and roast in the oven.

CARROTS There is no need to peel carrots, just remove the top and root end, give them a quick scrape with a sharp knife, and rinse in cold water. *To cook*: Start with cold water, bring to the boil, reduce the heat, and simmer gently for a few minutes until the carrots are *barely* soft, with a bit of crunch left.

CELERIAC (also called celery root) Wash, peel, and cut into chunks, or grate to have raw in salads (mixed with a little lemon juice to prevent discoloration). *To cook*: Bring to the boil, reduce the heat, and simmer for 15–20 minutes until tender.

ZUCCHINI Wash, cut off both ends, and discard. Depending on the size of the vegetable, cut into rounds, or cut lengthwise once or twice, then slice from one end to the other into halves or quarters. *To cook*: Sauté in oil or butter, or add straight to the pan in stir-fries and sauces (at the same stage as onions and/or peppers) and cook for 10–15 minutes until soft.

FENNEL Wash, trim, and slice lengthwise, or chop like an onion. The feathery bit at the top can also be chopped up and used in salads and sauces. *To cook*: Sauté in butter or oil for a few minutes until soft.

PUMPKIN (*see butternut squash*) *To cook*: Roast, boil, and mash, or grate raw pumpkin to make pumpkin muffins (page 189).

# NOTES

*Alcohol*

Some of the recipes in this book contain a certain amount of alcohol. I never worried about letting my children eat food cooked with wine, sherry, cider, or brandy, even when they were very young, but it's a personal decision, so put the alcohol in or leave it out. Whatever you think is right. If you don't buy much alcohol but like the idea of adding a splash of something to certain recipes I think sherry has more uses than anything else, in everything from soup to puddings. (Or you could buy miniature bottles of other liquors.)

### Salt

I never cook vegetables in salted water because I don't think it makes any difference to the flavor, especially if you add a little salt to your meal at the table, which is why a lot of these recipes don't include salt where you might expect to find it—in some of the sauces and most of the cakes, pastry, and batter mixtures for example. Again, it's a personal decision and I know lots of people can't bear to cook vegetables without salt, but don't overdo it with potatoes. They absorb a lot of salt from the water that you're better off without.

### Quantities

Unless stated otherwise, the quantities of vegetables and seasoning in each recipe are only approximate and can be adjusted any which way you like. (In some recipes specific quantities aren't given at all.) Where a "standard" can is mentioned this refers to the average, most common size, although the measurement given on the can could say 410g, 400ml, or 14 ounces. And where a recipe mentions just "a can" or "one can," this also refers to the standard size, unless stated otherwise.

### Servings

A rough guide to how many people each recipe serves is usually given, but in some cases this would just be too general—most soup, cake, and miscellaneous recipes (spreads for example)—so has been left out.

"All happiness depends
on a leisurely breakfast."

—John Gunther

# 1
## Wake up to breakfast

*Breakfast wasn't very exciting when I was a child; toast and cereal just about had it covered in our house, so once I started going to work early in the morning I dispensed with breakfast altogether and ate a couple of Kit Kats on the bus. Then I left home and breakfast became a cup of tea and a cigarette, followed by another cup of tea and a cigarette at the office. In fact, I didn't really take breakfast seriously until I was pregnant for the first time—and then it was a struggle to keep down one Weetabix.*

Lots of people, especially children, dread eating first thing in the morning, but endless research has shown how important breakfast is. Having witnessed the effects of going without food on tired, listless, and irritable kids, I agree that getting them to eat something before they leave the house makes a huge difference, not only to their happiness and well-being, but to the way they behave and perform at school, so it's worth getting into good habits as soon as you can.

There's nothing wrong with toast and cereal of course, but there are plenty of alternatives, so try and make breakfast a bit more interesting and less of a chore by making changes and finding out what your children like, what they don't like, and what they wouldn't eat if it was the only thing between them and total starvation.

If you want them to eat something they haven't tried before and you're not sure how they're going to react, give them the chance to try it first on the weekend or during the holidays, rather than on a school morning when you're pushed for time and already have a hundred-and-one things to worry about.

# EVERYDAY BREAKFASTS

## *Cereal*

I think it's fair to say you can separate cereal into two camps; the goodies, made entirely from whole grains with little, or no, added salt and sugar, and the baddies, which contain a lot of extra sugar, and in some cases as much salt as you'd find in a bag of chips.

I suppose any cereal has to be better than nothing because they all contain added vitamins and are eaten with milk (and if you get into the good habit of not giving children extra sugar from the very beginning, they'll never miss it). There's nothing to stop you reading the labels on every box in the supermarket if you feel like it but, as a general rule, the less fancy looking the cereal, the healthier it's going to be. Anything frosted, flavored, colored, coated in honey, or mixed with chocolate chips and other bits and pieces is certain to contain some or all of the things you want to avoid, so here's a quick guide to your best bets.

OATMEAL All oatmeal, any oatmeal; from a box, from a bag, or an individual package. There shouldn't be any added sugar in oat cereals, even the ones aimed specifically at children, and now quick-cooking oatmeal can be made in the microwave you don't even have the bother of cleaning the saucepan afterwards.

KELLOGG'S ALL-BRAN Greatly improved since the days when it tasted exactly like minced cardboard, but if you still can't bear to eat it on its own (I can't), make a delicious fruit and bran loaf instead (page 177).

SHREDDED WHEAT The bite-size version is especially good for kids, and this is one cereal that doesn't go soggy in the milk.

MUESLI With or without added sugar, there are so many healthy ingredients in muesli, does it really matter?

WEETABIX Make it more interesting for children by pouring on a fruit smoothie, or milk flavored with a spoonful of Nesquik, rather than plain milk.

### Fruit

If you haven't eaten fruit for breakfast before because you're worried you'll be starving long before lunch, give it a try; I bet you find a good helping of fruit (especially with yogurt) fills you up far more effectively than a bowl of soggy cereal.

In fact, fruit is a really easy option at breakfast time, especially in the spring and summer months, and I've found that even children who don't normally favor fruit often find a few slices of banana with a small spoonful of yogurt and honey less daunting than a piece of toast or a bowl of cereal. Not only does it look more inviting, it's nice to have something sweet when you've got a dry, early morning taste in your mouth. (If you're worried about brushing your teeth too soon after having fruit, eat a small piece of cheese to neutralize the acid in your mouth and protect the enamel, then wait a couple of minutes. The same rule applies anytime you've eaten food containing a lot of acid; I always gave my children a piece of cheese after a marathon sweet-eating session— of which there were many—and it seems to have worked for them so far.)

Just a few slices or chunks of fruit, or a combination of fruits, such as banana, apple, pear, melon, kiwifruit, grapes, or berries, with live-culture yogurt (plain or fruit) and a teaspoonful of honey drizzled over the top.

Half a grapefruit or an orange cut into segments and sprinkled with very little sugar. Put the fruit under the broiler to melt the sugar and take the chill off if you like, especially in the winter when cold fruit isn't so appealing. (If you buy the sweeter varieties of grapefruit you shouldn't even need to add sugar.)

Jarred prunes. Soft, sweet, and easy to eat. Most ready-to-serve prunes I've come across aren't even particularly wrinkled, despite what their bad reputation suggests. (Eat five, then if you do "Tinker, Tailor" with the stones, it always come out "rich man.")

Fruit smoothies. The possibilities are endless *(see Chapter 7: Can't Cook? Don't Cook!)*.

### Cake

Cake is the answer to a parent's prayers on those cold, dark winter mornings when it's an effort getting out of bed on time, no one fancies fruit, and you don't want to make anything more complicated than a cup of tea. When you think about it, plenty of Europeans with far fewer health problems than we have in this country eat cakes, croissants, and jam for breakfast all the time, and I don't see a problem as long as children have a small glass of milk or fresh juice with it.

Bran loaf, rock buns, fruit and muesli muffins, bread pudding, apple, ginger, carrot, or plum cake *(see Wholesome Cakes in Chapter 8: Let Them Eat Cake)* or cheese and zucchini scones (page 166) all do the trick.

### Eggs

Eggs are so versatile, and in their simplest forms they only take a very few minutes to cook.

BOILED EGGS Everyone has a theory on the best way to boil an egg, and now there's more than one gadget on the market to do the job for you. Assuming you're not spoiled enough to have your butler produce six boiled eggs in a row for you to choose from, all you have to do is start with cold water, a teaspoon of salt, and a drop of vinegar in the smallest saucepan you've got; then bring to the boil and simmer gently for 2½ minutes for a very soft boiled egg, with the white just firm and yolk very runny. If you're doing several eggs at once and everyone likes their egg a different way, follow the same procedure and remove all the eggs from the water at the same time. Eggs continue to cook in their shells, so take the tops off the soft eggs immediately; anyone who wants a harder egg can wait another two minutes while they eat a piece of toast, before taking the top off their egg.

POACHED EGGS I've tried poaching eggs in the microwave as well as in a pan specially designed for the job, but I still think the easiest way by far is just to break the egg into a cup and drop it straight into a saucepan of lightly salted, gently boiling water; about 2 minutes for a firm white and soft yolk, 3–4 minutes for a firm yolk.

OPEN HOUSE EGGS Warm enough oil to just cover the bottom of a frying pan; cut a hole in a piece of bread with a cup or glass and put both pieces of bread into the pan. Break an egg into a cup and drop it into the hole in the slice of bread. After a couple of minutes, flip everything over and fry for another couple of minutes. Squeeze tomato sauce onto the egg, replace the circle, and serve.

SCRAMBLED EGGS Add a good splash of milk to make the eggs go further (for me, scrambled eggs without milk are too rich anyway) and for speed, scramble them in a large, nonstick, shallow frying pan—as opposed to a regular, deep-sided saucepan—with a tablespoonful of melted butter.

## Avocado Sandwiches

Mash an avocado (or two, according to how many sandwiches you want to make), spread on buttered brown bread and cut the crusts off. Avocados are the perfect good mood food; nice and easy for little mouths to swallow first thing in the morning.

## Pancakes

If you can't bring yourself to make batter and get a pan dirty before breakfast on a school morning, make a stack of pancakes in advance and freeze them.

TO MAKE ABOUT A PINT OF BATTER (6–12 PANCAKES, DEPENDING ON THICKNESS OF PANCAKES AND SIZE OF PAN)
4–5 very heaping tablespoons all-purpose flour
2 eggs
1 cup (250 ml) milk

1. Sift the flour into a bowl or a large measuring cup (4 cups plus), make a well in the center, add the eggs and about half the milk, start whisking with a small hand whisk or fork and gradually add the rest of the milk. Thin with a little more milk if necessary. Transfer the batter into a measuring cup with a lip or a batter bowl, which will make it easier to pour into the frying pan.
2. The secret of perfect pancakes is a very hot pan and no surplus oil sloshing around, so warm enough oil to cover the bottom of the frying pan, then pour the excess oil into a clean cup so it can be used again, and give the pan a quick wipe with a paper towel.
3. Pour in enough batter to make a pancake, tipping the pan as you go to get the bottom of the pan covered as quickly as possible.

4. As soon as the surface of the pancake is completely dry, run a knife around the edge and turn it over, or toss it by holding the pan away from you, shaking the pancake towards the far end as far as it will go without falling out, and flipping it over in one deft movement. Pour a little more oil from the cup into the pan after every couple of pancakes, heat thoroughly, then wipe the pan almost dry with paper towels.

## TO FREEZE

1. Make the pancakes as described above, layer them with wax paper or plastic wrap when they've cooled (which only takes a few minutes), then put the whole lot in a large ziplock bag and freeze.
2. No need to defrost them; place each pancake on a plate—or two pancakes on one plate, a little apart—and microwave on high for 1–2 minutes.

## ALSO TRY . . .

Peanut Butter Pancakes.

I thought of making pancakes with peanut butter as a way of adding protein, otherwise pancakes can be a bit lightweight when you've got a busy day ahead and no way of knowing when you'll be able to eat again.

I use smooth peanut butter—it blends easily with the batter in seconds—but I don't see why you couldn't use crunchy peanut butter instead if you prefer it.

1. Make the batter in the usual way, with a bit less milk, and use a fork to whisk 2 teaspoons of peanut butter into the mixture at the end—roughly 1 teaspoon per 1 cup (250 ml) of batter. (Add more milk if the batter needs thinning.)
2. Make pancakes in the usual way and serve with slices of banana and maple or golden syrup.

# WEEKEND BREAKFASTS

Unless you're super-efficient and get up at the crack of dawn, some breakfasts are better left until the weekend.

### *Eggs Florentine*

Make a cheese sauce in the usual way: Mix a heaping tablespoon of flour with about 1½ tablespoons (25g) of melted butter in a saucepan, cook for a minute, then add approximately 1 cup (250 ml) of milk and a handful of grated cheese and whisk continually until the sauce thickens. Keep the sauce warm and cover with plastic wrap or a couple of tablespoons of milk to prevent a skin forming. Wash and cook the spinach, preferably in the microwave in a casserole dish with a lid, and poach the eggs in boiling water. Serve the eggs on a bed of spinach with the cheese sauce poured over the top.

### *Hash Browns, Bacon & Beans*

As an alternative to broiling or frying, place bacon on a lightly greased baking sheet with sides at the top of the oven and cook at 400°F (200°C) for about 20 minutes—no need to turn it over. If you're making hash browns, fry them lightly on both sides and finish them off in the middle of the oven, while warming the canned baked beans with tomato sauce up in a lidded casserole dish at the bottom. Needless to say, homemade hash browns are infinitely superior to their supermarket equivalent (page 210).

## The Healthiest English Fry up Possible

Cook sausages in the oven in a very large ovenproof dish (preferably Pyrex, it's easier to clean), adding the bacon about halfway through the sausages' cooking time. Put the baked beans and canned plum tomatoes in a casserole dish, cover, and bake at the bottom of the oven for 10 minutes after you put the bacon in. Half-fill a large saucepan with boiling water from the kettle and put it on a low heat while you make toast. Poach the eggs in the boiling water for a very few minutes, by which time everything should be ready—and that's it!

ALSO TRY ...
BAKED APPLES (page 139), KEDGEREE (page 73), and CHEESE & ONION TOMATOES (page 91).

"Ask your child what he wants for
dinner only if he's buying."

—Fran Lebowitz

# 2
# Little gems and tough cookies

*Feeding your children good food is every parent's obligation. In fact, we all come from a long line of parents who fed their children, so why now, when we're swamped with so much advice and information about our food and the number of fat grams and calories it contains, does hardly a week go by without another deeply depressing story about morbidly obese children whose parents can't, or won't, stop feeding them a nonstop diet of processed rubbish?*

Apparently American teenagers are the first generation to be less healthy than their parents, and I read recently that increasing numbers of children are becoming anorexic, some of them, unbelievably, as young as six- and seven-years-old.

But maybe it's not surprising that kids are resorting to starving themselves when so many adults are permanently stressed out and preoccupied with food. If the parents are anxious and confused—withholding treats with one hand and feeding their children processed rubbish with the other—while their teachers search their lunch boxes for illicit chocolate cookies and bags of chips, what are they supposed to think?

Constantly subjected to images of size zero models and the idealistic, unrealistic zeal of humorless healthy-eating gurus on one hand; continually bombarded by the message that junk food and carbonated drinks are cool on the other—is it any wonder that going without nourishment altogether is starting to seem like the only alternative to obesity in the minds of impressionable young children?

But despite this grim picture, you can count yourself lucky that you don't need to be an expert on *anything* to feed your children a healthy, balanced diet with very little money and hardly any time, even if you have a tiny kitchen, only three saucepans (one with an ill-fitting lid), and no fancy gadgets unless you count the garlic crusher. Although it sometimes feels like an uphill struggle, whether your children are little gems who eat whatever you put in front of them, tough cookies who seem to leave more on the plate than you put there, or, like most kids, a combination of the two, cooking real food is nowhere near as exhausting, tricky, or unrewarding as some people make it out to be.

Finally, and speaking from experience, it doesn't matter where or how you live, feeding your children good food and laying the groundwork for the healthiest possible future is something that every one of us has in our power to get right.

# FUSSY EATERS

There can't be many children who *don't* go through a fussy stage, whether it's one type of food they don't like, food generally (heaven help you), or a particular time of day when they don't seem to want to eat anything.

Whatever it is, it's not worth losing your temper over; all that does is frighten the child and make the situation worse. Be prepared to be patient, even if you're feeling anxious, and remind yourself that the important thing is to encourage your children to eat, and eventually enjoy food, without turning mealtime into a battleground, because if that happens you really will have trouble on your hands.

I've found there are two schools of thought when it comes to persuading kids to eat. Either talk to them about their food; let them know exactly what it is and where it comes from, or try and disguise whatever they don't like so they end up eating some of the right foods without realizing. It's a case of working out which way works best in your house, and at the risk of confusing the issue, you'll probably find it will be a little bit of both.

Just remember that children have seldom, if ever, starved themselves completely, or incurred any lasting damage to their health by refusing certain foods, even kids who exist on a diet of baked beans and jelly babies, or some other weird combination, for months at a time.

Of course it's better all around if they learn to like a wide variety of foods early on and, from a personal point of view, I don't see any harm in offering a reward in the form of a dessert, or a very few sweets after dinner every day if that helps. Having said that, it's a good idea to give fruit as a treat sometimes (especially in the summer months when the really good stuff is in season: strawberries, raspberries, cherries, peaches, and plums, among other things) rather than the more obvious sweet treats, so children don't differentiate between nutritious and "naughty but nice" things too soon, in which case they're naturally going to want the latter every time.

Like everything else in life it's a question of finding the right balance, so be firm without being too forceful and you'll soon be able to spot the difference between a child who genuinely dislikes something, and one who's just pushing his luck because he'd rather eat a bag of chips than a bowl of soup.

There's no better way for children to develop good eating habits than watching their parents eat and enjoy food, so eat together as a family whenever you can, or if the children are very young and have dinner earlier than you, at least stay in the same room, and preferably sit down with them so you can have a conversation and help them along if they're struggling.

Try not to fly off the handle when they refuse to eat something the first fifty-five times, and shower them with praise and admiration when they do try. It's easy to forget that children actually want to please their parents most of the time (children under the age of twelve anyway), so make them feel good about themselves and lay off the guilt. There'll be plenty of time for that later on when they're selfish, ungrateful teenagers who treat the house like a hotel and don't appreciate anything you've done for them.

*Tips*

*Impose strict limits on juice and banish carbonated drinks altogether, except for parties and special occasions.* I've lost count of the number of very young children I've seen guzzling vast quantities of drink, and then, to the surprise and despair of their parents, not being able to eat anything. Avoid giving small children anything to drink except water and a certain amount of milk for as long as possible, and if you must give them juice, dilute it with as much water as you can get away with. Even expensive, unsweetened fruit juice can damage their teeth and too much liquid sloshing around in their stomachs takes the edge off their appetite. Never serve soft drinks at mealtimes either, just a glass of water, with or without ice. If children are genuinely thirsty they *will* drink water, or very diluted fruit juice, no two ways about it. This is one area where it pays to be really ruthless. It's up to you to put your foot down.

*Keep portions small.* It's better to give a child a tiny amount so they can ask for more than put them off with too much food at the start.

*Whenever you want them to eat food they say they don't like, or just something new that they haven't tried before, make sure you also give them something you know they do like.* Tempt them with fries and they might just eat the other vegetables on their plate without complaining.

*Try not to separate food into "good" and "bad" or "adult" and "kiddie" food.* No matter what their age, eat at least some of the same foods as your children at every meal.

*Sometimes it's the texture of certain foods more than the taste that's putting your child off.* Make fruit and vegetable smoothies in a blender for them to drink through a straw.

*Keep trying new things and don't be afraid to re-introduce food they didn't like the first time around.* Getting your kids into good eating habits is like teaching them road safety. You don't bring the subject up once or twice at the beginning and assume they've learned it; you still say "mind the road" every time they go near it—even when they're old enough to drive on it.

*Some sweet treats are less harmful than others.* Give children small amounts of chocolate rather than hard, sugar-coated candy whenever possible. Fruit popsicles and plain lollipops are another good bet for a relatively harmless sweet treat. In fact, it's a good idea to keep popsicles in the freezer year-round for when your kids are very sick or down with the flu. Slowly sucking a popsicle helps keep them hydrated when they can't eat or they're constantly throwing up.

*Provide savory snacks.* Try dry cereal or a few cheesy crackers instead of chips.

*Never, ever give a young child a whole package of sweets or chips.* Split one package between at least three kids and give each of them a tiny amount in a small bowl. If you've only got one child and you're trying not to fall into the trap of eating all their leftovers, seal the package with tape or a bag clip immediately, then put it back in the pantry—and always buy the smallest packages in the first place.

*Use a favorite doll or teddy bear as a prop.* Whether you're potty-training, trying to get kids to take their medicine, or encouraging them to eat, there's nothing most very young children like more than a game involving a loved and trusted toy.

*Grow your own herbs or mustard and watercress in a pot on the windowsill.* Cook with children as an activity (*see Cooking with Children in Chap-*

ter 8: *Let Them Eat Cake, pages 164–175*) to get them interested in food and reduce the fear factor.

*Have other kids over to eat with your children regularly.* They socialize and learn to associate food with happy occasions, instead of seeing every mealtime as an obstacle that has to be overcome as quickly as possible.

*Separate the food on their plate.* Start with two piles, and let your children choose to eat just one of them. Meet them halfway and none of you will be left feeling like the loser.

## PACKED LUNCHES

How do you make a reasonably nutritious packed lunch that won't reduce your child to tears of boredom or have you branded an unfit mother? It's no joke.

Once upon a time, all we had to worry about was the odd spilled drink or a squashed sandwich. Now, providing children with a packed lunch every day without finding the rotten remains hidden under the bed six weeks later or falling foul of the Lunch Box Police is more hazardous than a trip to Mars—and put one of those in their lunch box at your peril.

Unless you're one of those lucky parents whose children's school prepares proper, decent food on the premises—or you couldn't care less—the chances are you'll find yourself making packed lunches at least some of the time for a good few years. And no, I don't think a Mars Bar is the answer either, but I don't buy the "one size fits all" philosophy of schools who invent ridiculous rules about what you can and can't feed your children as a smokescreen for the unpalatable truth, which is: the food they provide is often even less healthy than french fries and chocolate and they can't be bothered to address the problem any other way. (One teacher I know of at a very PC primary school, which has

"Healthy Schools Status," whatever that means, allows the children's lunch boxes to be kept right next to the radiator.)

I agree that if you can't be bothered to try and feed your children something healthy at least some of the time you deserve a kick on the backside, but most of us *do* care very much, and I don't think anyone is in a better position than the parents to predict what their children *will actually eat*. It's all very well advising people to pack fruit salad and sandwiches full of lettuce and tomato, but there's no getting away from it, fruit doesn't always taste so good in a plastic box, and salad sandwiches go soggy long before lunchtime, no matter what.

Children can be very conservative in their eating habits and it's frustrating if they insist on taking crackers and jam for lunch every day, but if they've had breakfast and you know they'll eat a proper meal later on, it's nobody else's business. Nor do I think it's necessarily a bad thing to pack a small bag of chips or a chocolate cookie in addition to the main course. I always gave my children chips and cookies on condition that they ate at least half the sandwich and a bit of fruit first, and if they didn't have time for the treat I always let them eat it later on. Of course you need a bit of trust for this to work, but as a veteran packed-lunch maker I believe it generally *does* work—and any lunch supervisor worth her salt will see to it that no child gets the wrapper off a chocolate cookie while there's an untouched sandwich or an apple in their lunch box.

I was a lunch supervisor some years ago and I saw lots of packed lunches that had obviously been lovingly prepared by health-conscious parents, but which also included chips, cookies, cakes, and other now strictly forbidden items. I also saw some truly *dire* lunches—a single slice of cold, soggy toast for example—which wouldn't break any of the new rules, but hardly qualifies as wholesome either. The other important point about rules and forbidden food is that whatever isn't allowed automatically becomes more desirable.

Another thing I've noticed over the years is that the way kids of all ages eat at home can be very different from the way they act in front of their friends, and let's face it, most lunchrooms aren't exactly conducive to eating in peace and comfort. Then there's the time factor, the lure of the playground, and the smell of school lunches to put them off, not to mention peer pressure, as in: *"Eugh, what is THAT? You're not eating it are you?"* I remember a ten-year-old girl telling one of my children that his mum didn't love him because he had store-brand chips in his lunch box instead of Walkers. Honestly. Another time I couldn't understand why my teenage son flatly refused to take smoked salmon sandwiches to school, which he loves, until, in a moment of sudden clarity I realized that eating dainty smoked salmon sandwiches at the local comprehensive was more likely to get him beaten up than going around with a sign on his back saying "punch me."

Let's be clear about one thing. When your children are in primary school, you do at least have half a chance to get it right. After that, peer pressure (especially with boys) kicks in so hard you'll be lucky if they eat or drink *anything* that isn't fizzy, fried, or covered in sugar. Then all you can do is hope for the best and make sure they still eat the right food at home, where you still have some influence.

### Tips

If you have to make sandwiches in advance, wrap them in aluminium foil and store them in the fridge.

Cut the crusts off if you think it helps—two sandwiches without crusts for older kids—it makes them easier to wolf down in a hurry, and they get to eat more of the best bit of the sandwich that way.

Prepare sandwich fillings the night before; mash tuna, grate cheese . . . then you're already halfway there in the morning.

Buy lots of plastic boxes with tight-fitting lids in a variety of shapes and sizes; they come in handy for so many things (see below).

Don't stick to the same old white sliced. Even if your kids have sandwiches every day you can make them more interesting by varying the bread, as well as the filling. Whole grain, rye, whole wheat, whole grain white, half-and-half, pumpernickel, crusty rolls, cheesy rolls, bagels, wraps, and croissants all work well with any of the following: cheese and pickle, canned tuna or salmon mixed with corn kernels and mayonnaise, ham and cream cheese, beef and watercress, avocado and bacon, slices of cold meatloaf and mustard . . .

Reduce the likelihood of a soggy outcome (slightly) by putting salad between two layers of filling, away from the bread. Even so, it has to be said that some salad stuff lasts better than others. I've never had much success with tomato and lettuce, but diced cucumber and peppers can be mixed with tuna and mayonnaise; also watercress or mustard and cress, and corn kernels.

Pack slices of tomato and cucumber or lettuce and spinach in boxes with tight-fitting lids to be added to sandwiches or rolls at lunchtime.

Avoid anything that will smell, spill, or spoil too quickly, especially in the summer. Egg sandwiches are out, and cartons of yogurt generally don't last the course—plus there's a good chance that the lid will be pierced by a sharp object, covering everything with the contents.

Compartmentalized lunch boxes can be good for keeping everything separate and therefore less liable to damage.

Try the old trick of packing a carton of juice straight from the freezer to keep everything else in the lunch box cool in the summer. By lunchtime, the drink will still be half-frozen and mushy like a Slush Puppie.

Instead of sandwiches try:

- Cold chicken drumsticks or homemade chicken nuggets with coleslaw (page 48).
- Sausage rolls (page 59) and potato salad (page 210).
- Hummus (page 207) or guacamole (page 207) with carrot sticks and tortilla chips.
- Cold pizza.
- Pasta mixed with tuna, diced cucumber, and whole kernel corn.
- Rice salad (page 84).
- For slightly older kids, fill a thermos with hot soup or pasta and tomato sauce. This is definitely too nerdy for most teenagers, and even if it does work you'll probably find yourself replacing the broken thermos at least once a term, but it's always worth a try.

Buy the smallest bananas, fun-size apples, and seedless grapes, which are much more appealing and less daunting to children (not to mention plenty of adults).

Apples and bananas can get boring when there's nothing very exciting in season, so provide sticks of carrot, celery, cucumber, and red and green bell peppers instead.

Don't forget dried fruit: raisins, prunes, apricots, dates, figs, and cranberries.

Bend the no chips or cookies rule with homemade cheesy shortbreads (page 165) and wholesome cakes (*see pages 176–189*).

Make fruit Jell-O in tiny plastic pots with tight-fitting lids the night before; they'll be set by the morning. (Give kids plastic spoons and forks if you find the contents of your cutlery drawer gradually disappearing without a trace.)

If your children are desperate for something sweet and there's no ban on chocolate at their school include a couple of squares of good dark chocolate in their lunch box to finish off with.

The very clever mother of one six-year-old boy I knew when I was a lunch supervisor used to leave funny little messages in his lunch box, encouraging him to eat his food and enjoy it. Plenty of mothers, myself included, can only marvel at such devotion and presence of mind (my children would never have been able to read my terrible handwriting anyway) but, hey, it's a good idea. Maybe it could work for you.

"But when the time comes that a man
has had his dinner, then the true
man comes to the surface."

—Mark Twain

# 3
# Make dinner, not excuses

## GROUND MEAT

Ground meat may be the poor relation of beef, pork, and lamb, but it certainly has its uses, not least because it's perfect for disguising large quantities of vegetables in. It's also very versatile and inexpensive and a good starting point for getting kids accustomed to the taste and smell of meat, assuming that's what you want to do.

Once again, as it's so affordable to begin with there's not much to be gained from buying the cheapest. However, regardless of what kind of ground meat you buy, you should always get rid of the extra fat by almost covering the pan with a lid once the meat is cooked, then tipping the pan and carefully straining off as much of the excess fat as you can. Liposuction for meat in other words—and if you haven't done this before you'll be horrified at the amount of extra fat you could have been swallowing. *Eugh.*

### *Tips*

Use a couple of cans of corned beef in Shepherd's Pie instead of ground lamb if you feel like something different.

Always dry-fry ground meat straight from the package; even if the label says "extra lean" it still contains more fat than you need.

Make leftover chili or Bolognese sauce go further by adding a couple of cans of chopped tomatoes and some more seasoning.

## Shepherd's Pie

Not long ago I read that when Jamie Oliver asked a young mum why she didn't make Shepherd's Pie for her kids she said it was "too posh."

Shepherd's Pie is a lot of things—delicious, cheap, and easy to put together year-round—but posh? I don't think so.

There's no end to what you can add to the meat in Shepherd's Pie, so try finely chopped celery, a handful of frozen mixed vegetables, spinach, grated carrot, whole corn kernels, or leftover vegetables (carrots, rutabaga, cabbage, or broccoli, for instance) cut into small pieces.

Instead of potato alone, use a mixture of potato and sweet potato or butternut squash for the topping; add an egg to make the potato drier and fluffier, or a spoonful of creamed cheese with minced parsley or chives, or just plain butter and milk.

Ground lamb is a bit more expensive than ground beef (although not that much), so if you can't get lamb or you want to use ground beef instead, just add plenty of rosemary. Hardly anyone will be able to tell the difference.

Serve with green vegetables, or just baked beans, and make extra gravy if you like.

SERVES 4–6
Potatoes: however many you think would make a serving of
    mash for each person
1 pound (450–500 g) ground lamb
1 onion, chopped
1 clove garlic
Mushrooms
Carrot, grated
1 lamb, beef, or vegetable stock cube, or 1 teaspoon of Marmite

Dried rosemary
Frozen whole kernel corn
Tomato paste
1 tablespoon instant gravy granules
A lump of butter
A splash of milk
Grated cheese (about ¼ cup/25 g)

1. Preheat oven to 375°F (190°C). Peel the potatoes, or scrub them and leave them in their skins *(see page 95)*, then cut them roughly into quarters and put them on the stovetop in a saucepan of fresh, cold water.
2. Dry-fry the meat in a very large pan over low heat, breaking it up with a wooden spoon now and then, while you get the vegetables ready.
3. Add the onion and garlic to the pan as soon as you like, then add the mushrooms and grated carrot, stirring every now and then until the meat is almost cooked and you can clearly see the fatty juices.
4. Strain off the excess fat *(see page 39)*, then crumble in the stock cube and add the rosemary, a couple of handfuls of frozen corn kernels, and a tablespoonful of tomato paste.
5. Add a tablespoonful of instant gravy granules to thicken and then simmer for a few minutes until the potatoes are ready. Transfer the meat into a large ovenproof dish.
6. Drain and mash the potatoes with a lump of butter and a splash of milk; add the grated cheese, then spread the potato topping over the meat, and bake for 15–20 minutes, or until the potatoes are brown and the gravy is bubbling.

# Moussaka

—————

SERVES 6
THE MOUSSAKA
1 pound (450–500 g) ground lamb
1 onion, finely chopped
2 cloves garlic, minced
1 lamb or beef stock cube
Tomato paste
1 teaspoon ground allspice
Very little water
4 medium to large potatoes
2 eggplants
Mushrooms

THE TOPPING
1 stick (8 tablespoons) (113 g) butter
2 cups (500 ml) warm milk
3 tablespoons all-purpose flour
2 egg yolks

FOR THE MOUSSAKA
1. Cook the ground lamb in a very large saucepan with the finely chopped onion and garlic for a few minutes, then strain off excess fat *(see page 39)*.
2. Crumble in the stock cube, add some tomato paste with the allspice and a little water, and stir well.
3. Meanwhile, peel the potatoes and bring to a boil in a pan of fresh cold water; reduce the heat and simmer until soft, then allow to cool for a few minutes before cutting into thick slices.

4. Cut the eggplants into thinly sliced quarters and soak in a bowl of salted water for 5 minutes while you peel and finely slice the mushrooms.

5. Drain the eggplant thoroughly and dry with a clean tea towel or paper towels, then deep-fry in very hot oil and set aside to drain on clean paper towels.

6. Put the fried eggplant in a bowl and mix with the sliced mushrooms. (The eggplant absorbs so much oil there's no need to fry the mushrooms as well.)

7. Layer the meat with the eggplant and mushrooms in a large ovenproof dish and finish with a layer of the sliced potatoes.

FOR THE TOPPING

1. Preheat oven to 350°F (180°C). Melt the butter in a saucepan and warm the milk in another saucepan, or in a large bowl in the microwave: about 4 minutes on high.

2. Add the flour to the melted butter in the saucepan and stir over the heat for a minute until bubbly, then pour in the warm milk, whisking continuously.

3. When the sauce starts to thicken, add the egg yolks and whisk for another minute.

4. Pour the topping over the moussaka and bake for 30–40 minutes until the sauce is bubbling and the topping has a golden crust.

## Chili con Carne

As usual, the quantities here are all approximate, so add more, or less of the vegetables, according to what you have and what you like best. The same applies to the amount of chili powder, cumin, etc. I always make more chili than I need and keep (or freeze) some, which is why there's more meat here than in most other ground meat recipes. In fact, the quantities below should be enough to make two meals (accompanied by pasta, rice, salad, and vegetables, etc.) for a family of four.

2 pounds (1 kg) lean ground beef
2 bell peppers, any color
2 zucchini
Mushrooms
1 large onion
Garlic paste
Chili powder
Pinch of curry powder
Ground cumin
Dried basil
Spinach
1 or 2 cans of plum (240 g) or chopped tomatoes (about 14.5 ounces/411 g each)
1 can kidney beans (about 14.5 ounces/411 g)
Tomato paste

1. Put the ground beef in a large, deep-sided pan over low heat and let it brown slowly while you wash and chop the vegetables. (Break up the lumps of meat from time to time with a wooden spoon.)
2. When the meat is just about cooked, drain off the excess fat (*see page 39*) and add the peppers, zucchini, mushrooms, onion, herbs, and spices and give it all a good stir.
3. Wash a generous handful of spinach and add to the meat with the canned tomatoes; keep stirring and increase the heat to make it bubble. Thoroughly rinse the kidney beans in a colander, drain, and add them in.

4. Add enough tomato paste to thicken the sauce until it's the way you like it, then reduce the heat, cover with a lid, and simmer very gently for about 30 minutes.

## Hamburgers

Use lean ground beef or buy the best steak you can afford and mince it in a blender or food processor at home. Add a finely chopped onion, a few herbs, and some bread crumbs if you want to stretch the meat a bit further. You don't need a huge amount of meat to make a good hamburger, especially if you top it up with lettuce, tomato, and real cheese (as opposed to processed slices, or that gunk from a plastic bottle . . . what exactly is that stuff, anyway?). Serve with chunky homemade fries.

MAKES 6 GOOD-SIZED BURGERS
2 pounds (1 kg) ground beef or minced steak
1 large onion, finely chopped
1 egg, to bind

OPTIONAL
Paprika or cayenne pepper
Black pepper
Parsley, finely chopped
Bread crumbs

1. Squish everything together in a large bowl and pat the mixture into burger shapes with your hands, making them as large and thin as you can without them falling apart.
2. For best results put the burgers under the broiler on the highest setting and broil on both sides for a few minutes until they're brown on the outside and just done in the middle.

## Rissoles

Rissoles were one of those things we used to joke about at school. All I really remember is that they were made with ground beef and rice (I think)—and I'm guessing bread crumbs. Anyway, this is how I make mine. Serve them hot with vegetables and a few potato wedges, or cold with salad and pita bread.

Use whichever kind of rice you like, and instead of beef, ground pork or lamb are also good.

MAKES APPROXIMATELY 10 LARGE RISSOLES
¾ cup (150 g) rice
2 eggs, beaten
¼ cup milk
2⅓ cups (200 g) fresh white bread crumbs
1 pound (450–500 g) ground beef
Seasoning
Salt and pepper
Oil, for frying

1. Preheat oven to 350°F (180°C). Cook the rice in the usual way, then strain through a sieve and immediately rinse with plenty of cold water.
2. Mix the beaten eggs with the milk and spread the bread crumbs out on a large, shallow baking sheet.
3. Put the cooked rice into a very large bowl with the raw meat (and whatever herbs and spices you want to use) and squish it together gently with your hands.
4. Shape into Scotch egg–size balls, or slightly smaller, dip each ball into the egg mixture, then coat with the bread crumbs.
5. Heat enough oil in a very large saucepan to just cover the rissoles (a piece of stale bread will turn golden in less than 30

seconds if the oil is hot enough) and deep-fry for a few minutes until the coating is crisp and brown.

6. Put the rissoles on a baking sheet and bake for about 20 minutes.

ALSO TRY . . .

BEEF & CHEESE CRUMBLE.

Make a crumble with 1¼ cups (150 g) all-purpose flour, 5 tablespoons (75 g) of butter, and ⅓ cup (25 g) of grated cheese for topping a casserole made with a family-sized package of ground beef, thoroughly cooked with onions, mushrooms, and corn kernels, then mixed with a thick gravy, seasoning, and a dash of Worcestershire sauce.

SPAGHETTI BOLOGNESE (page 251).

MEATBALLS Use up small amounts of uncooked ground beef to make tiny meatballs (page 62) for mixing with pasta and tomato sauce.

# CHICKEN

There's been a never-ending stream of bad publicity about chicken and turkey farming in recent years. Nevertheless it's still popular probably because, not counting sausages and burgers, children seem to prefer it to any other kind of meat.

I must admit I still love chicken and turkey and I think as long as you steer well clear of the dodgy stuff—by which I mean chicken from any fast-food outlet, the cheap brands in the supermarket meat case or freezer, and anything that isn't proven free-range—you should be fairly safe.

Just in case you haven't seen and heard enough hard evidence already about the horror that is cheap chicken, it's usually been farmed and handled in extremely unhygienic conditions, then pumped full of water and chemicals to increase the weight, which means you're paying more money for less (poor quality) meat.

Chicken dishes made from reconstituted meat, including the ones marketed for children, are even worse. Skin, fat, a whole host of other body parts, and cheap fillers are just a few of the things you could be swallowing every time you eat chicken Kiev or a slice of turkey roll, and although one of the manufacturers' favorite claims is "made with 100 percent breast meat," what they don't tell you is that the product only contains about 56 percent meat in the first place and that will be factory farmed and full of water.

## Chicken Nuggets

Not to be confused with the sort of nuggets, dippers, drumettes, or burgers you find in the supermarket. Call them what you will, they're all processed and very low in nourishment.

But don't give up on chicken nuggets altogether, make them at home instead. These chicken nuggets are made with real chicken breasts and, surprise, surprise, real chicken is exactly what they taste of. Don't be tempted to leave the carrots, apples, and onion out; not only do they make the chicken go further, they really do add flavor (and vitamins) and make the nuggets more tender and that much tastier.

MAKES APPROXIMATELY 20 GOOD-SIZED NUGGETS
2 large carrots
1 large onion
2 apples
2 boneless chicken breasts, skin removed
1 pound (450–500 g) (4 to 5 cups) fresh white bread crumbs
2 eggs beaten together with a little milk
Oil, for frying

OPTIONAL
Flour
Lemon juice
Dried tarragon or thyme
Salt and pepper

1. Roughly chop the carrots and onion, peel and core the apples, and cut the chicken into large pieces.
2. If you're using the above quantities, blend all the ingredients in a 2-quart food processor. If you've got a smaller food processor, or you're making twice as many nuggets, blend the chicken first, followed by the fruit and vegetables. (Although you can whiz everything to a smooth paste if you like, I prefer my nuggets to have a chunkier texture, so blend the ingredients on a slow setting, or pulse, to get the consistency you want. Alternatively, grate the fruit and vegetables by hand with a cheese grater and snip the chicken into tiny pieces with kitchen scissors.)
3. Put the blended ingredients into a large bowl and squish it all together lightly with your hands, adding some bread crumbs if you think the mixture is a bit wet.
4. Spread the bread crumbs across a large, fairly shallow oven-proof dish or baking sheet, and beat the eggs together in a bowl with about ½ cup (120 ml) of milk. (Coat the nuggets in flour before dipping them in the beaten egg mixture if you like; I don't bother.)
5. Shape the nuggets with your hands, dipping each one into the egg mixture first, and working with only a small amount of bread crumbs at a time to avoid making a mess of the whole baking sheet and creating too much waste.
6. To cook the nuggets: Warm enough oil, about 2 inches (5 cms), in a large pan to completely cover the nuggets. Test if it's hot

enough by dropping a small chunk of bread into the pan; it should turn brown in a matter of seconds. If the oil is too cool, the nuggets will break up and go soggy. Otherwise they will turn crisp and golden in about 1 minute.

7. Preheat oven to 350°F (180°C). Fry the nuggets, then place on a baking sheet and finish cooking them in the oven, for about 15 minutes until cooked through.

Note: *If you're freezing chicken nuggets, place them side by side (uncooked) on a small baking sheet, cover them with aluminium foil, and place them in a ziplock freezer bag, or layer them with wax paper in a plastic container and seal tightly with a lid. When you take them out, allow them to thaw slightly for a few minutes so they're easier to separate, remove excess moisture with paper towels, and for best results follow the cooking instructions above.*

## Chicken Curry

If you want a meatier curry, double up the amount of chicken and use the same quantity of vegetables.

SERVES 4–6
1 large onion
1 medium carrot
Mushrooms
4 boneless breasts chicken, skin removed
Oil
2 cloves garlic, crushed
1 cup chicken stock (made with stock cube)
Tomato paste
1 small carton plain yogurt, or 4 tablespoons from a big carton
1 sachet of coconut paste, or substitute some coconut milk

THE SPICES

2 teaspoons (plus) medium curry powder
1 teaspoon ground cumin
½ teaspoon ground coriander
½ teaspoon ground ginger

1. Preheat oven to 325–335°F (160–170°C). Wash and finely slice the onion, carrot, and mushrooms.
2. Rinse the chicken in cold water, dry well, and cut lengthwise into narrow strips.
3. Warm some oil with the crushed garlic and spices in a very large saucepan and quickly fry the chicken pieces for a couple of minutes.
4. Reduce the heat and add the onion, carrot, and mushrooms, making sure everything is coated with the spices.
5. Pour in the stock and tomato paste, followed by the yogurt and coconut, and stir well.
6. Cover with a lid and cook gently for up to an hour, stirring occasionally, or transfer the curry to a casserole dish with a lid and cook in the oven for the same amount of time.
7. Serve with plain boiled rice.

## Mexican Chicken

The Tex-Mex seasoning you get with DIY taco kits tends to be made with chili powder, coriander, and cumin, so if you have all these spices in your pantry already, it's cheaper and more convenient to make your own. (And as a rough guide, I'd say one medium-sized chicken breast makes two wraps.)

I like those long, thin, sweet red peppers for this, but any peppers will do. (Add a chili pepper if you like it hot.)

To make 6
3 boneless chicken breasts, skin removed
Oil
1 each, small red and green bell peppers, thinly sliced
1 small onion, thinly sliced
Tortilla wraps, flour wraps, or taco shells

The seasoning
4 teaspoons ground cumin
4 teaspoons ground coriander
1 teaspoon (plus) medium chili powder
Salt and pepper

1. Wash the chicken well and cut lengthwise into thin strips.
2. Mix the seasonings together on a dinner plate and coat the meat (you can always make more if you run out) or, if you prefer, add the spices to the hot oil.
3. Heat the oil in a large pan and quickly fry the chicken.
4. Reduce the heat, add the thinly sliced peppers and onion, and cook for a few minutes until soft.
5. Serve with shredded lettuce and thinly sliced tomato and cucumber in wraps or taco shells, or with plain boiled rice and guacamole.

## Chicken & Ham Pasta Bake

This only takes a few minutes longer than a pasta bake made with a jar of instant sauce, and apart from having a far superior flavor it also contains a lot less salt.

If you don't have tomato juice, use two cans of chopped tomatoes or a carton of passata (finely chopped and strained tomatoes) instead.

I only use two chicken breasts to save money, but there's no reason why you can't use more chicken than this without making any other alterations to the recipe.

SERVES 4–6
2 boneless chicken breasts, skin removed
Olive oil
1 onion, chopped
1 clove garlic, minced
Mushrooms, sliced
½ package (about 5 slices), honey roast ham, chopped
2 teaspoons rosemary, or mixed herbs
3 cups (¾ liter) tomato juice
2 heaping tablespoons soft cream cheese (or Quark) (about
    8 ounces/240 g)
Dried pasta shapes (about 1 handful per person)
2 handfuls of grated cheese (a mix of mozzarella and cheddar is
    good)
1 package salted chips, scrunched up in the bag

1.  Preheat oven to 350°F (180°C). Cut the chicken breasts into strips or small pieces. Warm a little olive oil in a large pan. Fry the chicken gently with the onion and garlic for a few minutes.
2.  Add the mushrooms and ham, followed by the herbs, tomato juice, and cream cheese, stirring for a few minutes until the cheese has blended thoroughly into the tomato sauce.
3.  Put the uncooked pasta into the pan with the sauce, mix well, then pour everything into a large ovenproof dish, making sure all the pasta is covered with sauce.
4.  Top with the grated cheese and scrunched up chips and bake for 30–40 minutes, by which time the pasta should be perfectly cooked.

## Sweet & Sour Chicken

With couscous instead of rice, this is very nearly a quick fix. If you want to make it with pork instead of chicken you'll need to cook the meat a bit longer, simmering for 20–30 minutes instead of 10, once the sauce has been made.

SERVES 6
4 boneless chicken breasts, skin removed
All-purpose flour
Oil
1 onion
1 red bell pepper
1 orange or yellow bell pepper
1 standard can pineapple rings (about 8 ounces/227 g)
2 tablespoons vinegar (malt, white, or white wine)
2 tablespoons tomato paste
2 tablespoons soy sauce
1 rounded tablespoon sugar (light brown or white)

1. Wash and cut the chicken into strips or small pieces and coat in a little flour.
2. Warm some oil in a large saucepan.
3. Fry the chicken on all sides, then reduce the heat and cover with a lid while you finely chop the onion and peppers.
4. Add the chopped onion and peppers to the pan. Drain the pineapple and reserve the juice. Cut 3 or 4 pineapple rings into small pieces and add them to the chicken followed by the vinegar, tomato paste, soy sauce, sugar, and all the reserved juice from the can of pineapple.
5. Stir well, cover with a lid, and simmer very gently for about 10 minutes.

ALSO TRY . . .

Chicken in Cream & Mushroom Sauce.

Coat chicken thighs in a little flour or chicken seasoning (plan on about two pieces of chicken per adult), then fry in butter and olive oil, adding crushed garlic, finely chopped onions and mushrooms, seasoning—mixed herbs, grained coriander, and nutmeg are all good—and about 1 cup light cream. Simmer gently for about 25 minutes while you make boiled rice and a mixed salad.

Chicken Goujons.

Make chicken breasts into chicken *goujons* by cutting them lengthwise into long, thin strips, dunking in beaten egg and bread crumbs, and deep-frying, as you would with chicken nuggets.

# SAUSAGES

Poor old sausages have come in for a lot of bad press in recent years, and let's face it, some of them deserve their bad reputation, especially if the horror stories about what goes into them are to be believed; cows' eyeballs and pigs' snouts are two of the less repulsive ingredients I've heard about.

Sadly, I have to say I do believe the stories—and once again, the worst examples I've come across were in primary school lunches. As a rough guide, go for sausages that contain an absolute minimum of 70 percent meat, and preferably 80 percent plus (you'll see from the ingredients listed on the back of the packaging) and don't be tempted by the cheaper ones. It's not worth it.

## Toad in the Hole

Always, *always* use all-purpose flour for Yorkshire pudding—if you use self-rising you'll get a flat, solid result—and make sure the oil is at least *sizzling*, if not *smoking* hot when you pour the batter in; that's the secret of perfect Yorkshire pudding. Some people say you should make the batter in advance and rest it in the fridge for a while, but I don't think it makes a lot of difference. All-purpose flour and hot oil are the magic ingredients—and use 2 eggs instead of one, even for smaller quantities of Yorkshire pudding; that way your pudding will have more substance and stay firm and well-risen, instead of shrinking up and losing its perfect shape a few seconds after you take it out of the oven.

As a rough guide, use one heaping tablespoon of flour per person and add the milk gradually so you can see where you are with it before you make the batter too thin and have to start sifting in more flour.

SERVES 4
8 English-style sausages
Oil
1 cup (120 g) all-purpose flour
2 eggs
½ cup (125 ml) milk

OPTIONAL
1 small onion, finely chopped

1. Preheat oven to 400–425°F (200–220°C). Arrange the sausages evenly in a large ovenproof dish with some extra oil. (The sausages make their own fat, but you need more to cook the Yorkshire pudding in; an extra 3–4 tablespoons

should do it.) Prick the sausages a few times with a sharp knife and put them in the preheated oven. If you're using the onion, chop it finely and scatter around the sausages after about 10–15 minutes when the oil is hot and the sausages are starting to go brown.

2. Now sift the flour in a largish mixing bowl (give yourself plenty of elbow room) and make a well in the center.

3. Break the eggs into the well one at a time; add about half the milk and start whisking, gradually adding more milk until you've got a fairly thick, smooth, pouring batter (add even more milk a little at a time if the batter is still too thick). You can leave the batter in the fridge, but have it ready to pour into the very hot oil the minute you remove the sausages from the oven.

4. When the sausages are brown and very nearly done, quickly pour the batter into the dish and return it to the top half of the oven immediately. After about 20 minutes, you should have lovely dark brown sausages and perfect golden, well-risen Yorkshire pudding.

## Cider Sauce for Sausages

According to traditional recipes you're meant to cook the sausages in the sauce for part of the time, but I don't see the point unless you like your sausages soft and soggy. I think it works better to cook the sausages separately (in the oven, or broil them) and just pour the sauce over them on the plate at the end.

Use mushrooms and sweet red bell pepper instead of carrots if you prefer, in which case you'll only need to simmer the sauce for about 20 minutes instead of half an hour.

MAKES 1½–2 CUPS
1 onion
2 carrots
2 celery stalks
Butter
Oil
2 tablespoons all-purpose flour
½ cup (125 ml) beef stock
2 cups (450ml) medium-dry apple cider
1 bouquet garni
Parsley, chopped
Salt and pepper

1. Chop the onion, carrots, and celery as finely as you can. Warm the butter and oil in a large saucepan and saute the vegetables until the onion is soft and slightly golden.
2. Stir in the all-purpose flour and cook for another minute, then add the stock and the cider along with the bouquet garni and bring to the boil.
3. Reduce the heat and simmer for 30–40 minutes, or until the carrots are just soft, adding parsley and seasoning to taste.

ALSO TRY . . .
Jamie Oliver–Style Pan-Fried Sausages.
Split sausages in half lengthwise, open them up, and fry them flat for cooking in double-quick time.
Sausages in Curry Sauce.
Use up leftover curry sauce (or a jar of ready-made if you're desperate) by reheating in the microwave and pouring over well-done sausages and plain boiled rice.

# PORK

## Tips

For the very best crackling, roast a joint of pork with the rind on for the first hour, then remove the rind and cook separately at the top of the oven.

Don't waste time making applesauce; store-bought apple-sauce or a large jar of organic baby apple puree does the same job.

## Sausage Rolls

Sausage rolls are usually made with puff pastry; too tricky and time-consuming for most of us to tackle at home, so I make sausage rolls with suet which is dead easy to handle—even for very inexperienced pastry makers—and which, contrary to popular belief, actually contains less saturated fat than butter.

These sausage rolls are especially nice hot (they're perfect with mashed potatoes, green vegetables, and gravy), but are also good cold and keep well in the fridge for quite a few days.

MAKES APPROXIMATELY 12 SAUSAGE ROLLS
THE FILLING
1 pound (450–500 g) ground pork
1 package poultry seasoning mix
1 jar chunky style apple sauce or 1 large jar of baby apple puree

## THE PASTRY
2 cups (225 g) self-rising flour
4 ounces (100 g) suet
¾ cup (175 ml) water

1. Preheat oven to 375°F (190°C). Put the pork, seasoning mix, and chunky applesauce (or puree) in a large bowl and squish it all together with your hands.
2. Mix the flour and suet together in another bowl and gradually add the water to form a ball of dough. The dough should be quite soft, but firm enough to handle easily; if it's too sticky, sprinkle more flour into the mixing bowl and keep kneading gently until it feels right.
3. Roll the dough out on a floured surface into a large rectangle; as thin as you can get it without tearing.
4. Form the sausage meat into a fat roll, roughly the same length as the pastry, and place in the middle. Fold one side of the pastry across the meat and brush with milk. Bring the opposite side of the pastry over, pressing it down gently to hide the seam, then brush the top and sides of the giant sausage roll with milk, trim the rough ends, and cut it crosswise into slices. You should get about a dozen sausage rolls roughly 2 inches thick.
5. Place the sausage rolls on a greased baking sheet and bake for 20–25 minutes, until the pastry is a deep golden brown.

## Sweet Apple & Apricot Pork

Serves 4–6
The Pork
4–8 pork tenderloin medallions
2 small apples
Dried apricots (about a handful)
1 red onion
Oil

The sauce
1 teaspoon all-purpose flour
1 teaspoon butter
2 teaspoons dried sage
½ cup (250 ml) pork or vegetable stock (made with 1 stock cube)
1 tablespoon golden syrup

1. Preheat oven to 350°F (180°C). Trim any excess fat from the pork. Wash and finely chop the apples, apricots, and onion.
2. Warm enough oil to just cover the bottom of a large pan and quickly fry the pork with the finely chopped onion, turning once.
3. Place the pork and onion in a large ovenproof dish and cover with the apples and apricots.
4. Blend the flour, butter, and sage together in a large measuring cup to make a smooth paste. Add the stock cube, syrup, and 1 cup (250 ml) of boiling water, and whisk with a fork or small hand whisk until everything has dissolved.
5. Pour the sauce over the pork and cover the dish with a lid or a sheet of aluminium foil.
6. Cook for about an hour, or until the pork is tender.

## Ginger Beer Pork

SERVES 4–6

Oil

1 pound (450–500 g) pork tenderloin

2 tablespoons all-purpose flour

Salt and pepper for seasoning the flour

1 onion, thinly sliced

1 clove garlic, crushed

1 cup (250 ml) pork or vegetable stock

1 cup (250 ml) ginger beer

2 teaspoons brown sugar

1 teaspoon caraway seeds

1. Warm some oil in a large saucepan while you cut the pork into thin strips and coat lightly in the seasoned flour.
2. Quickly fry the pork; drain the oil if it's a bit dirty, and add some fresh oil to the pan with the onion and garlic.
3. Stir in the stock and the ginger beer (page 215) with the sugar and caraway seeds; bring to the boil, then reduce the heat and simmer very *gently* for 45 minutes to an hour, until the pork is tender. Serve with any combination of winter vegetables and lots of mashed potatoes.

## Spicy Pork Meatballs

The quantities given below make at least 30 tiny meatballs, so if you don't need this many now, freeze some—or cook the lot and put the leftovers in a salad the following day. It's a bit fiddlier making the meatballs this small, but for my money they work better as jawbreakers than ping-pong balls.

MAKES 30 TINY MEATBALLS
1 pound (450–500 g) ground pork
1 large egg
¾ cup (63 g) bread crumbs
6 tablespoons flour (all-purpose or whole wheat)
1 tablespoon curry powder
1 tablespoon ground cumin
Black pepper
Oil, for frying

1. Put the meat in a large bowl and squish it up with the egg and bread crumbs.
2. Sift the flour and spices onto a large dinner plate.
3. Roll the mixture into balls and coat in the seasoned flour.
4. Shallow-fry the meatballs in very hot oil for 10–15 minutes and serve with a tomato sauce *(see DIY Pasta Sauce, page 93)* and either rice or pasta, or mashed potatoes.

ALSO TRY . . .
PORK IN PLUM SAUCE.
Quickly brown some pork tenderloins in a pan, then transfer to a casserole dish, cover with a lid, and cook in a slow oven, pre-heated to 325°F (160°C) while you stew 1 pound (500 g) of plums in a saucepan with a little water, 1 level tablespoon of light brown sugar, ½ teaspoon of cinnamon, and ½ cup of red wine. After 15 minutes when the plums are soft, push them through a sieve, pour the puree over the pork, and continue cooking for about 1 hour until the pork is tender.
GREEK-STYLE PORK.
Cut pork tenderloin into strips and sear the meat in a large saucepan with very hot oil. Cover with a lid and simmer gently

for 30–40 minutes, then add half a small bag of torn up spinach, 1 teaspoon of nutmeg, and ½ large carton of plain yogurt mixed with 1 tablespoon of all-purpose or whole wheat flour. Stir well and simmer gently for another 10 minutes. Serve with pita bread and salad.

# BEEF

## *Tips*

Use kitchen scissors for cutting up raw meat; it's much quicker and more hygienic than messing about with knives and chopping boards.

Stir in a spoonful of mustard straight from the jar to give beef dishes an extra kick, or make a casserole with 1 cup (250 ml) of stout instead of beef stock and cook slowly for 1½–2 hours until the meat is tender.

## Beef Stroganoff

Usually made with tenderloin, a cheaper and equally good version can be made with rump or braising steak; all you need to do is cook the meat a bit longer.

SERVES 6
1½–2 pounds (about 1 kg) steak
Oil
Butter
1 medium onion
½ pound (225 g) button mushrooms, sliced
1 teaspoon mustard, preferably Dijon

2 tablespoons sherry or brandy
⅔ cup (150 ml) light cream
Parsley, chopped

1. Cut the steak across the grain into fine strips and sprinkle with a little salt and pepper. Heat some oil in a large frying pan, and saute the meat for a minute to seal on all sides. Reduce the heat and cook the steak on low heat for about half an hour.
2. Add a lump of butter to the pan and fry the finely chopped onions until soft and golden, then add the sliced mushrooms and cook for another 2 or 3 minutes.
3. Stir in the mustard with the brandy (or sherry) and cream, and warm through very gently (to prevent the cream curdling) for 5–10 minutes.
4. Sprinkle with plenty of parsley and serve with plain boiled rice and salad.

ALSO TRY . . .
Beef Curry.
Make curry with stewing steak instead of chicken (*see Chicken Curry, page 50*), slow-cooking the meat for an extra 15–20 minutes at the start, before you add the vegetables and make the sauce.

# LAMB

## Lancashire Hot Pot

Lancashire hot pot was traditionally made with lamb chops or cutlets on the bone; as succulent and juicy as the most expensive leg of lamb. (*See also Scotch Broth, page 126.*)

SERVES 6
2 pounds (1 kg) potatoes
Oil
1 large onion, chopped
2 pounds (1 kg) lamb chops or steaks
Dried thyme
Dried rosemary
Salt and pepper
2 cups (500 ml) lamb or beef stock
Butter

1. Preheat oven to 350°F (180°C). Peel the potatoes, rinse them well, and slice into rounds about ⅛ nch (2mm) thick.
2. Heat some oil in a large pan, fry the onion for a few minutes, then add the lamb and brown the meat quickly on all sides.
3. Put half the potato rounds on the bottom of a deep oven-proof dish, cover with the lamb and onions, and season well with the herbs and salt and pepper.
4. Pour in the hot stock, then layer the rest of the potatoes on top of the meat and dot with small pieces of butter.
5. Cover the casserole with a lid, or a sheet of aluminium foil, and cook in the oven for about 2 hours, then remove the lid and continue cooking for another 15–20 minutes until the potatoes on the top are golden brown and crisp around the edges.

ALSO TRY . . .
Kebabs.
If you have meat left over from a roast lamb, this is the perfect way to enjoy a guilt-free kebab without risking your health and wondering what, exactly, is inside that festering thunder-thigh rotating on the spike in your local kebab shop. Simply reheat the

meat by frying quickly in very hot oil, then turn the heat down, cover with a lid, and keep warm while you wash some salad and warm the pita bread under the grill. Make a great spicy mint sauce by blending the following ingredients together, in no particular order, and mixing with the cooked lamb. (For a thicker sauce just add more yogurt.)

2 tablespoons plain yogurt
1 tablespoon vinegar
1 teaspoon mint
1 heaping teaspoon sugar
½ teaspoon curry powder
½ teaspoon turmeric
½ teaspoon salt

Medallions of Lamb in Red Wine.
Slice approximately 1½ pounds (600 g) loin of lamb into medallions and brown the meat in a pan with butter and olive oil. Add a finely chopped red onion, mushrooms, and half a bottle of red wine, then simmer for about 45 minutes, or until the meat is tender. Thicken the sauce with a little cornstarch mixed with a couple of spoonfuls of liquid from the pan, plus a small spoonful each of gravy granules and tomato paste. Serve with boiled new potatoes, or mashed potatoes, and green vegetables.

# LIVER

Raw liver is never a pretty sight. Right up there with Brussels sprouts and lumpy custard, it's one of those things that lots of children, not to mention adults, go green at the mere mention of. Not only that, you have to spend at least ten minutes preparing liver before cooking it and you run the risk of splattering blood all over the kitchen if you plonk a plateful down too care-lessly on the work top. So what then, is the point of liver?

Well, if you can get past the downside, liver is also pretty tasty, versatile, full of protein—and dirt cheap. Calves liver or beef liver is your best bet for an everyday dinner, closely followed by chicken livers. Calves' liver is tender and delicious, but slightly more ex-pensive, so even though it's my favorite I only buy it occasionally.

To prepare liver: Put the liver into a colander and give it a good rinse under the cold tap to get rid of most of the blood; now you can see the skin and any other little bits of sinew that need removing much more easily. (As with any other meat, I find it much easier to cut liver up with kitchen scissors.) Coat the pieces in a little seasoned flour and you're ready to go.

## Chicken Liver Risotto

Add a half-glass of white wine and half-teaspoon of cayenne pepper with the stock for extra zing.

SERVES 4–6
1 onion
1 clove garlic
2 bell peppers
1 zucchini
Mushrooms
½ pound (250g) chicken livers
4 strips of bacon, or Irish bacon
Oil
Rice (about one handful per person)
2 cups (500 ml) chicken stock (made with 2 stock cubes)
Dried thyme
Parsley, chopped

A handful of spinach
Paprika
Salt and pepper

1. Wash and chop the onion, garlic, peppers, and zucchini; slice the mushrooms.
2. Prepare the liver in the usual way; snip into small pieces with the bacon, and quick-fry for a few minutes in a large saucepan with the oil until the bacon is brown and crisp and the liver is done on the outside.
3. Strain off as much of the oil and liquid as you can; warm some more oil in the pan, then add the onion, garlic, peppers, and zucchini and cook for a few more minutes, until the onion is soft and golden. Add the sliced mushrooms and cook 1–2 minutes more.
4. Wash and drain the rice, mix it well with the meat and vegetables in the saucepan and add the stock with the herbs. (Don't worry too much about any extra liquid; risotto tends to be wetter than most other rice dishes and you can always strain some of the liquid off at the end once the rice is cooked if you think there's too much.)
5. Cover the saucepan with a lid and simmer very gently for about 15 minutes until the rice is just soft, adding the spinach about 5 minutes before the end. Sprinkle the finished risotto with paprika and season to taste with salt and pepper.

ALSO TRY . . .
Liver, Bacon & Onion (page 246).
Liver in Black Bean Sauce.
Prepare and pan-fry 1 or 2 packages of liver with a sliced red onion, then add a small can of pineapple chunks, drained, and the black bean sauce. Stir well and simmer for about 15 minutes.

Spicy Liver & Pork Meatballs.
Add 1 small package of roughly chopped liver to about 1 pound (450 g) of ground pork (page 62).
Mixed Grill.
A great favorite back in the 1970s when shrimp cocktails and Black Forest Cake were the height of fashion, a mixed grill is traditionally a fat- and cholesterol-laden time bomb. Make a slightly less lethal version by washing and preparing the liver in the usual way, then frying in a little olive oil and butter with some kidney, mushrooms, and a small, finely sliced onion. Garnish with watercress and serve with good quality, oven-baked sausages, broiled tomatoes, and potato wedges or oven fries.

# FISH

Support your local fishmonger—or the fresh fish counter in your local supermarket, if you're lucky enough to have one. I think lots of us tend to be unadventurous when it comes to buying and cooking fish simply because we just don't know what to do with it and are too shy to ask. Native fish stocks have been in crisis for a long time and by now we should all be eating more sustainable fish. So don't ignore those friendly, helpful faces behind the fish counter any longer; ask for advice and start cooking more fish from this moment on. I will if you will.

### Tips

Shrimp can be defrosted much more quickly than the instructions on the packaging suggest if you're using them for cooking. Just put them in a colander and rinse well in cold water; leave to drain for about 15 minutes, then rinse well again.

## Tuna Lasagne

If you like, use grated cheddar instead—although cottage cheese makes this a very low-fat option—and leave out the parmesan and bread crumb topping.

Serve with salad, broccoli, or any other green vegetables, and extra corn.

SERVES 4–6
Spinach (a couple of handfuls)
1 can tuna (any size)
Frozen shrimp (1 small bag or half a large one), defrosted
2 standard cans chopped tomatoes (about 14.5 ounces/411g each)
Frozen whole kernel corn or one small can
Lemon juice
Dried basil
Black pepper
Lasagne sheets (about 9)

THE CHEESE SAUCE
½ stick (4 tablespoons) (56 g) butter
⅓ cup plus 1 tablespoon (50 g) all-purpose flour
2 cups (500 ml) milk
1 small carton cottage cheese

OPTIONAL
Bread crumbs
Parmesan cheese

1.  Preheat oven to 350°F (180°C). Wash the spinach and tear into pieces. Drain the can of tuna and mix with the defrosted

shrimp, chopped tomatoes, corn, lemon juice, and seasoning in a large bowl.

### FOR THE CHEESE SAUCE

1. Melt the butter in a large saucepan, stir in the flour and cook for a minute until the paste is glazed and shiny looking.
2. Remove from the heat, add the milk and cottage cheese, and return to the heat. Keep stirring the sauce continuously and make it easy on yourself by using a small hand whisk instead of a wooden spoon to prevent it from lumping. (If you want the sauce a bit thinner, just whisk in more milk.)

### THE ASSEMBLY

1. In an ovenproof baking dish, layer the tuna mixture and the pasta sheets with a couple of spoonfuls of cheese sauce, finishing with a complete layer of cheese sauce on the top.
2. Sprinkle the top with bread crumbs and grated Parmesan cheese. Bake for 20–30 minutes until the sauce is bubbling and the top is a deep golden brown.

## Sweet & Spicy Shrimp

SERVES 4–6

2 red or orange bell peppers
1 small can baby corn
3–4 broccoli florets
Oil
Sesame seeds
2 tablespoons light brown sugar
½ cup (125 ml) hot water
Tomato paste
Garlic paste

Soy sauce
1 level teaspoon chili powder
1 large bag frozen shrimp, defrosted
2–3 shredded wheat–style squares of dried noodles, or nests of
   noodles.

1. Cut the peppers lengthwise into thin strips, slice the baby corn
   whichever way you want, and chop the broccoli into tiny florets.
2. Heat the oil in a wok or very large saucepan. Stir-fry the vegetables in the hot oil for a few minutes with the sesame seeds.
3. Meanwhile, dissolve the light brown sugar, and 1 tablespoon
   each of tomato and garlic pastes in a ½ cup (125 ml) of boiling water. Add the soy sauce and chili powder and mix well.
4. Pour the liquid into the pan, turn up the heat, add the shrimp,
   and cook for another few minutes until everything is hot and
   the vegetables are just tender.
5. Break the dried noodles up a bit and add at the same time as
   the shrimp, otherwise leave the noodles out altogether and
   cook some white long-grain rice instead.

## Kedgeree

Kedgeree is traditionally a breakfast dish, but there can't be many
people who can eat this much food first thing in the morning.

Use whatever type of rice you like; I use brown rice and add
sesame seeds to give it a nice, nutty flavor—and this is yet another dish you could easily sneak spinach into if you wish.

Kedgeree may sound unexciting at best and pretty revolting at
worst, but it's actually lovely, tasty, and warmly satisfying. Hopefully
even your kids will like it. Over the years I've perfected my tech-
nique to the point where the whole thing takes less than half an
hour and requires hardly any cleanup. What more could you ask for?

SERVES 4–6
Brown rice (about 1 handful per person)
3–4 eggs
Smoked mackerel
3 or 4 scallions, or 1 regular onion
1 clove garlic
A small handful frozen peas
Oil
Sesame seeds
½ teaspoon curry powder
Parsley, chopped
Lemon juice

1.  Put the rice in a large saucepan with a generous amount of slightly salted water, stir, pop the eggs in, and put the pan on the stove over a high heat. Bring to the boil; boil rapidly for a minute, then turn the heat down low and cover with a lid.
2.  Meanwhile, prepare the smoked mackerel by removing the skin and checking carefully for bones. Flake the fish in a bowl then finely chop the scallions and garlic.
3.  After the eggs have boiled with the rice for about 10 minutes, remove them from the saucepan with a slotted spoon, set them aside, and add the frozen peas to the boiling water. Increase the heat until the water boils again, then reduce the heat and simmer for about 5 minutes, or until the rice is ready. (Don't let the rice overcook and go soggy.)
5.  While you're waiting for the rice, peel the hard-boiled eggs and cut them into wedges. Warm the oil in a large pan or a wok.
6.  Strain the cooked rice and peas through a colander and pour freshly boiled water from the kettle through the colander to remove any trace of starch.
7.  Fry the scallions, garlic, sesame seeds, and curry powder in

the warm oil until the onion starts to soften, then add the fish and cook for another minute or two.

8. Add the rice and peas, hard-boiled eggs, and plenty of parsley, mix well. When you're sure it's warm enough, sprinkle with lemon juice and serve.

## Fish cakes

MAKES 12 LARGE FISH CAKES
6 frozen white fish fillets, or 2 large fresh
4 fairly large potatoes
Butter
Milk
1 standard can tuna (about 5 ounces/142 g)
1 small can whole kernel corn
Lemon juice
Black pepper
½ pound (225 g) fresh whole bread crumbs (about 2¾ cups)

1. Cook the fish in an ovenproof dish, according to the instructions on the packet (or for about 10 minutes if using fresh fish).
2. Meanwhile, boil the potatoes—with or without the skins—before mashing them with a tablespoonful of butter and some milk.
3. Use a slotted spoon to transfer the fish to a mixing bowl and flake with a fork, then drain the cans of tuna and corn and add them to the bowl with lots of lemon juice and black pepper.
4. Add the mashed potatoes to the bowl, mix well, then form into fish cakes with your hands.
5. Gently press the fish cakes into a baking sheet of bread crumbs on both sides (you don't have to dip them into beaten egg

first unless you want to) and fry in a large saucepan for a few minutes, with enough hot oil to completely submerge the fish cakes. Keep warm in the oven and serve with French fries or potato wedges and green vegetables or a salad.

ALSO TRY . . .
Fastest-Ever Fish Cakes (page 108).
Fish Pie.
Use a mixture of white fish, canned tuna, and shrimp mixed with lemon juice, seasoning, ½ glass of white wine, and a basic cheese sauce made with 2 tablespoons flour, 2 tablespoons (56 g) butter, 1 cup (250 ml) of milk, and ⅓ cup (50 g) of grated cheddar cheese; top with mashed potato, and cook in the oven for 20 minutes, until the potato browns and the sauce bubbles.
Broiled Sardines.
Melt 2 tablespoons (56 g) of butter in a saucepan and stir in 1 teaspoon each of coriander, paprika, sugar, and Tabasco sauce; make a series of shallow diagonal cuts on both sides of the fish from head to tail, coat the fish, and broil for about 5 minutes on each side, turning once.

# (MOSTLY) VEGETARIAN

## Tips

Use aluminium foil *shiny side inwards* to direct more heat towards the food.

Eat shoots and leaves; packages of mixed stir-fry vegetables are a good value and you can add extra mushrooms, peppers, bean sprouts, or onions according to taste.

## Stuffed Peppers

Life may be too short to stuff a mushroom, as Shirley Conran famously said, but it's definitely not too short to stuff peppers. If you're using very large peppers you'll probably only need one each, otherwise make it two small peppers per person.

SERVES 4–6
4 large bell peppers, mixed colors
1 onion, or a few shallots
4–6 mushrooms
Butter
Olive oil
2 cloves garlic, minced
1 teaspoon ground cumin
1 teaspoon mixed spice
8 ounces (225 g) couscous
1 package Quorn pieces

OPTIONAL
1 vegetable stock cube
Grated cheese

1.  Preheat the oven to about 400°F (200°C). Slice the tops off the peppers, remove the stems and membranes. Wash the tops and the whole peppers inside and out. Stand the peppers up in a deep roasting pan.
2.  Finely chop the onion, mushrooms, and tops of the peppers and fry in a large pan with butter and olive oil. Add the garlic, cumin, and mixed spice and give it a good stir.
3.  Meanwhile, add the boiling water to the couscous in a large

bowl (according to the instructions on the package), stir, cover, and for a few minutes.

4. Now add the Quorn to the pan with the vegetables, and if you want more liquid, crumble in the stock cube, if using, and add a drop of water.

5. Fluff the couscous up with a fork and mix with the vegetables and Quorn.

6. Stuff the peppers, piling any remaining mixture loosely around the base. Cover the pan loosely with aluminium foil (*see Tips, page 76*), bake for 20–30 minutes, removing the foil for the last 5 minutes, and sprinkle the peppers with grated cheese, if using.

## Stuffed Mushrooms

On second thought, stuffed mushrooms make a great starter or side dish and go very well with rice and salad . . .

1–2 large flat cap stuffing mushrooms per person
1 stock cube
Garlic paste
Goats' cheese (a couple of ounces), crumbled
White bread crumbs (a couple of handfuls)
Parmesan cheese
Olive oil
Parsley, chopped

1. Remove the stems then wash and peel the mushrooms—or don't peel and wash the mushrooms; peel but don't wash, or wash but don't peel—some people say you should, some say you shouldn't. (For what it's worth, I usually do both.)

2. Dissolve a stock cube in a small saucepan of boiling water, and poach the mushrooms for a few minutes.

3. Put the warm mushrooms on a baking sheet or broiler pan, spread each one with a spoonful of garlic paste topped with crumbled goats' cheese and a mixture of bread crumbs and Parmesan cheese. Drizzle with olive oil and broil for a few minutes until the toppings are crusty and brown. Sprinkle with chopped parsley.

## Veggie Burgers

You don't really need an egg to bind the mixture together but put one in if you like or used a beaten egg mixed with melted butter to glaze the burgers instead of oil. Use whatever spices you like—coriander, cayenne pepper, and curry powder are all good. Normally, I'm against the idea of smothering food in tomato ketchup, but veggie burgers are one of the few things that really do taste better with lots of it.

MAKES 6–8 BURGERS (DEPENDING ON SIZE)
2 onions
2 carrots
1 zucchini
Olive oil
2 cloves garlic, crushed
Dried thyme
1 can chickpeas (about 14.5 ounces/411 g)
6 tablespoons oatmeal
Tomato paste
Salt and pepper
Whole wheat flour

OPTIONAL
1 egg, to bind

1. Preheat the oven to 400°F (200°C). Finely chop the onions. Grate the carrots and zucchini.
2. Warm some oil in a pan; fry the onion, carrots, and zucchini over medium heat and add the crushed garlic and thyme.
3. Meanwhile, drain the chickpeas and mash them up a bit with a fork in a large bowl.
4. Put the oatmeal in the bowl with the chickpeas, and as soon as the vegetables have softened, throw them in as well.
5. Add a couple of squirts of tomato paste, salt and pepper, and 2 tablespoons olive oil and mix it all together.
6. Shape the mixture into burgers using your hands and the whole wheat flour and place on an oiled baking tray. Brush the burgers liberally with more oil and bake them for about 15 minutes.

## Eggplant Lasagne

To make a lasagne for more than six people, increase the amount of onion and eggplants, and make the cheese sauce with 3 ounces each of butter and flour and 1¾ pints of milk. (You don't need to increase the amount of cheese; a little goes a long way.)

Alternatively, make an eggplant bake by omitting the lasagne sheets and using one can of tomatoes instead of two.

Serve on its own, or with extra green vegetables, whole kernel corn, or a mixed salad.

SERVES 4—6
1 large or two smaller eggplants
1 onion
¼ bulb fennel

Oil

2 cloves garlic, crushed

Parsley, chopped

2 standard cans chopped tomatoes (about 14.5 ounces/411 g each)

½ cup (125 ml) vegetable stock

6–9 lasagne sheets

THE CHEESE SAUCE

2 tablespoons (56 g) butter or margarine

2 tablespoons all-purpose flour

2 cups (500 ml) milk

⅓ cup (25 g) grated cheese

1. Wash and thinly slice the eggplants, cut the slices in half, and put them in a bowl of salted water (*see Notes, page 13*).
2. Slice or chop the onion and fennel and fry in the oil with the crushed garlic and a good sprinkling of parsley.
3. Add the canned tomatoes and vegetable stock to the pan; bring to the boil, reduce the heat, and simmer gently while you fry the eggplant.
4. Heat more oil in another pan and, to save time, fry the eggplant slices on one side only, then drain them on paper towels.

FOR THE CHEESE SAUCE

1. Preheat oven to 400°F (200°C). Melt the butter in a large saucepan, stir in the flour, and cook for a minute until the paste is glazed and shiny looking.
2. Remove from the heat, add the milk and cheese, and return to the heat. Keep stirring the sauce continuously and make it easy on yourself by using a small hand whisk instead of a wooden spoon to keep it from getting lumps. (If you want the sauce a bit thinner, just whisk in more milk.)

3. Layer the lasagne sheets, tomato sauce, eggplant, and cheese sauce in a large ovenproof dish, finishing with a layer of cheese sauce on the top. Bake for 15–20 minutes.

## Lentil Moussaka

SERVES 6
THE MOUSSAKA
1¼ cups (225 g) green lentils or mung beans
Olive oil
1 onion, finely chopped
2 cloves garlic, finely chopped
1 standard can chopped tomatoes (about 14.5 ounces/411 g)
2 cups vegetable stock
2 teaspoons dried basil
1 teaspoon ground allspice
4 medium-large potatoes
2 eggplants
Mushrooms (6–8 depending on size)
Tomato paste

THE TOPPING
1 stick (8 tablespoons) (113 g) butter
2 cups (500 ml) warm milk
3 tablespoons all-purpose flour
2 egg yolks

FOR THE MOUSSAKA
1. Soak the lentils the night before according to instructions on the package.
2. Preheat the oven to 350°F (180°C). Heat a couple of tablespoons of olive oil in a very large saucepan. Add the finely

chopped onion and garlic and cook for a few minutes until the onion starts to brown.

3. Add the lentils, chopped tomatoes, and stock along with the herbs and spices and bring to the boil.

4. Boil quite rapidly for about 5 minutes, then reduce the heat and simmer very gently for about 1 hour, or until the lentils are soft and mushy.

5. Meanwhile, peel the potatoes and bring to a boil in a pan of fresh cold water. Reduce the heat to medium-high and cook until done, then drain.

6. Cut the eggplants into thinly sliced quarters and soak in a bowl of cold salty water for 5 minutes while you peel and finely slice the mushrooms.

7. Drain the eggplant thoroughly on paper towels or a clean, dry tea towel, then deep-fry in very hot oil.

8. Put the fried eggplant in a bowl and mix with the sliced mushrooms.

9. Slice the boiled potatoes. Add about half a tube of tomato paste to the lentils and stir well.

10. Layer the lentil mixture with the eggplant and mushrooms in a large ovenproof dish and finish with a layer of the sliced boiled potato.

FOR THE TOPPING

1. Melt the butter in a saucepan and warm the milk, either in another saucepan, or in a large bowl in the microwave (about 4 minutes on high).

2. Add the flour to the melted butter in the saucepan and stir over medium heat for a minute until bubbly, then pour in the warm milk, whisking all the time.

3. When the sauce starts to thicken, add the egg yolks and whisk for another minute.

4. Pour the topping over the moussaka and bake for 30–40 minutes, or until the sauce is bubbling and the top is golden.

## Rice Salad

Use whichever type of rice you like, but I think the lighter, fluffier texture of basmati rice is better suited to rice salad than brown or short-grain rice.

Change the salad ingredients around to suit yourself and add some diced chicken, ham, prawns, flaked tuna, or smoked salmon—this is another good meal for using up leftover bits and pieces.

In fact, there's only one thing you need to be absolutely certain of—as with any dish containing cold rice—and that's making sure you cook and store it in the right conditions. Because of the starch, warm rice is a haven for the sort of bacteria that can lead to a very nasty stomach upset—or worse.

To avoid trouble, strain the cooked rice in a colander then immediately rinse under cold running water for a minute; absorb the excess moisture with plenty of paper towels, and if you're keeping it for later, get the rice covered and into the fridge as quickly as possible. If you're cooking a lot of rice and you only want to save some of it, separate the rice you're planning to keep and follow the above procedure—just don't leave it sitting around in the kitchen for any length of time.

Finally, if you want to warm up cold rice, do it thoroughly, preferably in a pan with very hot oil, until it's piping hot.

1¼ cups (225 g) basmati rice
Baby corn
Sugar snap peas
Leftover cooked chicken breast meat

A few slices of cold ham
1 avocado
Baby plum tomatoes
2 scallions
Chives
Salt and pepper
Olive oil

1. Cook the rice in a saucepan of boiling water, boiling rapidly for a couple of minutes, then reduce the heat to low and simmer gently for about 10 minutes (don't walk away and do something else; you don't want it mushy and overcooked).
2. Strain the cooked rice through a colander; rinse with plenty of cold water, remove excess water with paper towels, put the rice in a large bowl, and cover loosely with a clean cloth or a sheet of aluminium foil. (No need to keep it in the fridge if you're planning to eat it straightaway; rice salad is one of those things that tastes better at room temperature than it does chilled.)
3. Just cook the baby corn and sugar snap peas (preferably in the microwave) so they still have plenty of crunch, and add to the rice.
4. Chop the leftover chicken and dice the ham. Halve the avocado and cut it into chunks Dice the plum tomatoes. Slice the scallions. Chop the chives. Then add everything to the bowl of rice with the seasoning, using whatever herbs you wish, and a little olive oil.
5. Stir gently, to blend everything together without turning it to mush, and serve.

## Nut-Free Nut Roast

This is more or less the same as the Curried Nut Roast *(see page 252)*. If you can't find a bag of mixed seeds in the supermarkets, buy smaller packages and mix them up yourself.

SERVES 6–10
Fresh bread crumbs made with 4–5 slices of white bread (about
  1¼ cups/105 g)
½ pound (225 g) mixed sunflower, pumpkin, and sesame seeds
1 can chickpeas (about 14.5 ounces/411 g)
1 large onion
2 smallish bell peppers (red/orange and green)
1 clove garlic, crushed
Olive oil
Sunflower/corn oil
1 carrot, grated
2 rounded teaspoons curry powder
1 rounded teaspoon ground coriander
Tomato paste
2 eggs, beaten

1. Preheat oven to 400°F (200°C). Make the bread crumbs in a blender or food processor, then put them in a very large mixing bowl.
2. Blend the seeds and chickpeas for about half a minute and add them to the bowl.
3. Meanwhile, chop the onion and peppers and fry with the crushed garlic in a mixture of olive oil and sunflower or corn oil, until the onion is crisp and golden.
4. Add the fried vegetables to the bowl with the grated carrot,

curry powder, coriander, 1 tablespoon of tomato paste, and the beaten eggs and mix thoroughly—use a fork, it's easier—to bind everything together.

5. Press the mixture into a well-greased, standard-sized loaf pan long-strip-lined with parchment paper (see *Lining the Pan, page 160*). Bake for about half an hour, until golden.

## Pizza

Contrary to what you may think if you've never made pizza dough before, this is as easy as falling off a log. True, you have to wait a little while for the dough to proof, but so what? If I make pizza I usually do it on a Saturday afternoon so we can eat it in front of the TV in the evening, so pick a time when you don't have to rush off anywhere else for a few hours.

As with most recipes where you get to play with dough, the whole process is a lot of fun and the results are at least as good as anything you get from a pizza parlor, let alone a supermarket.

If you've got enough pans (or 7-inch layer cake pans) and plenty of oven space you can make individual round pizzas, but I make mine in the same standard-size rectangular baking pan I use for a jelly roll (*see Notes, page 190*) and cut them up into squares; usually six large pieces per baking sheet.

THE QUANTITY BELOW MAKES ENOUGH FOR 2 LARGE, THIN AND CRISPY-TYPE PIZZAS AND 1 SMALL ROUND ONE (SEE ABOVE)—OR 2 LARGE PIZZAS AND 12 DOUGH BALLS.
THE DOUGH
1 pound (450 g) all-purpose flour
2 teaspoons (or 1 package) active dry yeast
1 teaspoon salt

1 teaspoon sugar
1 cup (250 ml) warm water, mixed with 2 teaspoons olive oil

1. Mix the dry ingredients together in a large bowl and make a well in the center.
2. Pour the warm water and oil into the well and quickly mix everything together with your hand to make a soft dough, then turn the dough out onto a floured surface and knead it well for a good 5 minutes, sprinkling more flour whenever you feel you need to.
3. Place the dough in a large, greased ovenproof bowl, cover with a damp tea towel, and place at the bottom of the oven on the lowest setting for about half an hour, until the dough has risen and doubled in size.
4. Place the dough on a floured surface and knead it again for another 5 minutes (this is known as knocking back).
5. Put the dough back in the oven to proof again, covered with the damp cloth (which you'll probably need to wet and wring out again) for about half an hour—same as before—until it has doubled in size, then knead the dough again for roughly 5 minutes.
6. Divide the dough into however many pieces you think you're going to need and roll out each piece to more or less the right size and shape for the pan you're using. Gently press the dough into the oiled pan, trim any rough edges, and brush the entire surface of the dough with a little more oil. Cover with plastic wrap and keep in the fridge until you've got all your bases ready and prepared the toppings, and your pizza is ready to go in the oven.

Note: *If you have enough dough left over, put it back in the oven covered with the damp cloth for another half an hour, then knead it again and either make* another pizza, or wrap it in plenty of plastic wrap and put it in the freezer. Alternatively, use leftover dough to make dough balls; just form the dough into ping-pong size balls, bake on a greased baking sheet at the bottom of the oven, and serve with garlic butter.

## THE PIZZA TOPPINGS

Anything goes really. I usually make one vegetarian and one meaty pizza on the baking sheets and mix whatever I've got left over to make the small round pizza, which goes something like this:
Any or all of the following:

1 onion, cut in half and thinly sliced
Green and red bell peppers, thinly sliced
Mushrooms, sliced
Spinach
Whole kernel corn
Tomato

Leftover cooked sausages or frankfurters
2–3 slices ham
2 strips bacon
Leftover meatballs
Leftover Bolognese sauce or chili con carne

Tomato paste
1 bag grated mozzarella cheese
Mixed herbs
Cayenne pepper

1.  Preheat oven to 400–425°F (200–220°C). Fry the onion and peppers and divide between two bowls; one meat, one veggie.

2. Fry the mushrooms and spinach, drain a small can of whole kernel corn, and add to the veggie bowl. Slice the tomato and set aside.
3. Chop up the leftover sausages, ham, etc. and add to the meat bowl.
4. Thinly spread all pizza bases with tomato paste, add the toppings, cover liberally with the grated mozzarella, top with sliced tomato. Sprinkle with herbs and spices and bake for about 20 minutes, changing the baking sheets over from top to bottom about halfway through the cooking time.

### Baked Potato Pizzas

Eternally popular, it's pizza again; this time on a potato base. *(See also Bread Roll Pizzas, Chapter 10: Weekly Menu Planning, page 249.)*

Use the largest baking potatoes you can get; one half should be more than enough for most children (and some adults). Cut the potatoes in half first to reduce the cooking time; prick each potato several times with a sharp knife then either wrap each half in aluminium foil and bake in the oven or start them off in the microwave by putting them cut side down on a plate and cooking on high for a few minutes before wrapping in foil and finishing in the oven.

Largest baking potatoes
1 red or orange bell pepper, chopped
Sliced scallions
1 small can whole kernel corn
Parsley, finely chopped
Chives, finely chopped
Salt and pepper
Chopped tomatoes

Butter

Grated cheese: a mixture of mozzarella and cheddar is good

1. Preheat oven to 350°F (180°C). Bake the potatoes in the usual way, then scoop out as much of the soft inside as you can without tearing the skin and causing a total collapse.
2. Put the mashed potato into a bowl with the chopped peppers and scallions, corn, herbs, seasoning, a couple of tablespoons of chopped tomatoes, some butter, and half the grated cheese and mix it all together. Season with salt and pepper.
3. Stuff the potato skins with the filling, top with the remaining grated cheese, and bake the potato pizzas for about 20 minutes until the pizzas are warmed through and the cheese is brown and bubbly.

## Cheese & Onion Tomatoes

Cheese & Onion pie without the pastry; these are great with sausages or bacon and beans for dinner, or as a very filling weekend breakfast. You don't have to feel guilty about discarding the insides of the tomatoes either; keep them in a sealed container in the fridge for a few days and use them up in any recipe that includes chopped tomatoes; chili, lasagne, shepherd's pie, or a pasta sauce.

SERVES 4

4 large beefsteak tomatoes

½ onion

1 teaspoon all-purpose flour seasoned with salt and pepper

⅔ cup (50 g) fresh white bread crumbs

2 ounces (50 g) grated cheese

½ cup (125 ml) milk

2 eggs, beaten

1. Preheat oven to 400°F (200°C). Using a very sharp knife, cut a circle out of the top of each tomato large enough to enable you to get the knife inside.
2. Discard the tops and use the knife to scrape out some of the tomato to make a hole large enough to fill.
3. Finely chop the onion and coat with the seasoned flour, then mix the onion in a bowl with the bread crumbs, grated cheese, milk, and beaten eggs.
4. Put the tomatoes in an ovenproof dish and spoon the mixture into each one (the amounts given here are enough to fill four beefsteak tomatoes to the top). Bake for about 30 minutes until the tops are firm and golden.

## VEGETABLES

If you only buy fruit and vegetables in season, you'll never be disappointed. (It's not that difficult either when you think about it.) What's the point of eating apricots and plums in January if they taste like polystyrene? And there's nothing to beat local strawberries from the beginning of June till the end of July, so try and resist those bright orangey-red imports you find in the shops year-round; most of the time they're as hard as bullets and taste of nothing.

### Tips

Ripen avocados by putting them in a brown paper bag with a banana for a few hours. Also ripen mangoes in a paper bag without the banana.

For perfect roast potatoes: Russet or Yukon Gold are best. Always parboil the potatoes first, simmering for no more than 5 minutes while you heat the fat in a large ovenproof dish. Strain the water off and bash the potatoes up a bit by shaking them two or three times in the saucepan with the lid on so they're soft enough on the outside to absorb some of the hot fat, which is what makes them lovely and crisp.

Poach mushrooms in stock made from Marmite instead of frying in butter when you want to cut calories.

Cook all your vegetables in one large saucepan; put the carrots in first (in cold water), then add broccoli or cauliflower with peas or corn, which only need 3 or 4 minutes, when the carrots are half-cooked. Or buy a vegetable steamer, which makes it easier not to overcook vegetables.

Make gravy by adding the vegetable water to gravy granules, for extra vitamins.

## DIY Pasta Sauce

Like Ratatouille (page 95), this pasta sauce is miles better than any of the bottled ones you find in the supermarket. Make it in larger quantities whenever you can so you've got some left over to freeze for another time. (The quantities below make enough for a main meal—with pasta—for about six people.)

DIY Pasta sauce is very versatile, so try these alternatives, or make up your own:

Add a dash of balsamic vinegar or a pinch of cayenne pepper for a spicier flavor.

For a creamy pasta sauce, stir a small carton of soft cream cheese, Quark, or crème fraîche into the sauce at the end.

Butter
Olive oil

2 onions

2 zucchini

2 bell peppers (any combination of red, green, orange, or yellow)

Mushrooms

2 cloves garlic, crushed

1 vegetable stock cube

Dried oregano or Italian herbs

Dried basil

1 standard can plum or chopped tomatoes (about 14.5 ounces/411 g)

Spinach (about half a bag)

½ glass red wine

Tomato paste

1.  Gently warm butter and oil in a very large pan while you wash and chop the vegetables the way you like them. (If you're planning to blitz the finished sauce in a blender, don't bother finely chopping the vegetables, just hack them to bits.)

2.  Put the garlic and all the vegetables except the spinach into the pan, cook for a few minutes until soft, then crumble the stock cube in with the herbs, add the canned tomatoes and spinach and give it all a good stir.

3.  Turn the heat up and let the sauce sizzle before adding the red wine and tomato paste. If you think the sauce is too watery after a couple of minutes, reduce it by cooking on high heat until the excess liquid evaporates, then reduce the heat and simmer very gently for a few minutes. To thin the sauce, add more vegetable stock and/or red wine.

## Ratatouille

SERVES 6 AS AN ACCOMPANIMENT TO A MAIN MEAL
Olive oil
1 onion, chopped
2 cloves garlic, crushed
1 eggplant
2 zucchini
1 red bell pepper
1 green bell pepper
Dried basil
Dried mixed herbs
2 standard cans chopped tomatoes (about 14.5 ounces/411 g
    each)
Tomato paste

1.  Heat some olive oil in a very large saucepan; add the onion
    and crushed garlic and cook gently for about 5 minutes.
2.  Meanwhile, remove both ends of the eggplant and zucchini;
    slice thinly into rounds, halves, or quarters, then soak the
    eggplant in a bowl of cold salted water for a few minutes be-
    fore draining well and drying with plenty of paper towels.
3.  Dice the bell peppers and put all the vegetables in the pan
    with the herbs, chopped tomatoes, and a little more olive oil.
4.  Give it all a good stir, bring to the boil, then reduce the heat,
    adjust the seasoning, and add however much tomato paste
    you think it needs.

ALSO TRY . . .
Skinny Mash.
Don't peel potatoes; just give them a quick wash with a brush in
cold water, then boil and mash them in their skins. Known as

skinny mash in our house, it saves a lot of time and is much nicer than it sounds.

Broccoli Cheese.

Make cauliflower cheese with broccoli instead of cauliflower, or a combination of both, and serve with pasta, crispy bacon, and broiled tomatoes.

Honey and Ginger Glazed Carrots.

Fry ½ pound (225 g) of thinly sliced carrots in some butter for a few minutes; add a cup of ginger beer and 2 teaspoons each of honey and brown sugar, bring to the boil, and simmer for a few minutes until the carrots are just soft.

Roasted Vegetables.

Any combination of mushrooms, onions, or shallots, squash, peppers, and finely sliced carrots sprinkled with sesame seeds, basted in olive oil, and roasted in a large ovenproof dish for about 30 minutes.

"We may find in the long run that
tinned food is a deadlier weapon
than the machine-gun."

—George Orwell

# 4
# Quick fixes

*The ultimate in speed and simplicity; to qualify as a quick-fix a recipe should take no longer than 20 minutes from fridge to table . . .*

## Tips

Make a stop-gap version of tomato ketchup with 2–3 tablespoons of tomato paste, 2 teaspoons vinegar, 1 teaspoon of brown sugar, and ⅔ cup (150ml) of boiling water. (Should be enough for four people.)

To make cold, hard butter straight from the fridge spreadable, pop it in the microwave on defrost for about 40 seconds.

For a crunchy, low-calorie snack, wash half a bag of curly kale in cold water, sprinkle with salt and vinegar (or any other seasoning you like), and pop into a hot oven on a baking sheet for about 10 minutes.

For fries that taste fried without the hassle of frying (and fewer calories) scrub and cut potatoes lengthwise into wedges, drizzle the oven fries with a little oil, and give them a good shake before you put them in the oven, then again halfway through the cooking time. (Or spice them up by mixing a tablespoon of curry paste or pesto with some hot oil on a large baking sheet first.)

Look out for tips and recipe ideas on packaging; you'll find them on everything from lentils and ready-made soups and sauces to packages of cookies, canned fruit, and Jell-O.

Freeze wine that's past its best (assuming you ever have any) in an ice cube tray or freezer bag to be popped straight into soups and casseroles when you need it.

## Pacific Pie

Everyone seems to have their own version of Pacific Pie so feel free to adapt the basic recipe—a couple of cans of tuna, some kind of sauce, and plenty of potato chips—to suit yourself. However you make it, it shouldn't take longer than five minutes at a snail's pace.

SERVES APPROXIMATELY 4
Broccoli, or spinach
2 large cans tuna (about 5 ounces/142 g each)
1 small can whole kernel corn
Grated cheese (English Red Leicester is perfect, but cheddar or
    mozzarella will do)
1 standard can chopped tomatoes (about 14.5 ounces/411 g)
Plain yogurt
Lemon juice
Black or white pepper
2 bags salted potato chips

1.  Wash and break up the broccoli or spinach into small pieces and put in a covered dish in the microwave with a drop of water. If you haven't got a microwave, put the broccoli in a small saucepan with enough boiling water to cover it and simmer for a couple of minutes. (If you're using spinach, it can go straight in with the rest of the ingredients.)
2.  Drain the cans of tuna and corn and put them in an ovenproof dish.
3.  Add the broccoli or spinach, a handful of grated cheese, chopped tomatoes, and a couple of spoonfuls of yogurt, the lemon juice, pepper, and whatever other seasoning you want to use and mix it all up.
4.  Crush the potato chips and sprinkle on the top of the pie with

more grated cheese and bake in a 400–425°F (200–225°C) oven at for 10–15 minutes.

ALSO TRY . . .

1. Instead of canned tomatoes and yogurt, use any, or a combination of any of the following, to make the sauce: a can of condensed soup, crème fraîche, mayonnaise, tomato paste.
2. Include canned broad beans and peas, or frozen mixed vegetables and bell peppers.
3. Instead of tuna, use a can of salmon, or one can each of salmon and tuna.

## Noodles

You can't go wrong with noodles, they're dirt cheap and keep for ages. Kids seem to love them and it's easy to mix them up with healthier ingredients.

SERVES 4–6
Butter
6 slices back bacon, or Irish bacon
Mushrooms (about 4–6 large)
Sesame seeds
Spinach (about ¼ bag)
½ cup (125 ml) vegetable or pork stock
¼ teaspoon nutmeg
White pepper
8 ounces (250 g) package dried egg noodles
Parsley or chives, chopped

1. Melt the butter in a large saucepan, snip the bacon into small pieces, and fry with the sliced mushrooms and sesame

seeds until everything is golden brown and the bacon is crisp.

2. Wash and tear the spinach up and add to the pan with the stock, nutmeg, and pepper, stirring well.
3. Break the dried noodles up, add them to the pan, and stir again.
4. Simmer for about 5 minutes, until the noodles are just soft. Serve sprinkled with parsley or chives and a small lump of butter.

## More Noodles

This is a good way of using up spare sausages and leftover, un-cooked, ground meat.

SERVES 4 MEDIUM-SIZED CHILDREN
2 sausages plus about 4 ounces (100 g) leftover ground meat—or a bit of both.
3 tablespoons flour, seasoned with salt and pepper
½ zucchini, cut into thin quarters
Onion, chopped
Olive oil
1 standard can chopped tomatoes (about 14.5 ounces/411 g)
¼ teaspoon cayenne pepper
Dried basil
Dried sage
Spinach (about ¼ of a bag)
2–3 squares dried rice noodles, or nests of noodles

1. Roll the meat into tiny balls, about the size of a quarter. If you're using leftover sausages, squeeze the meat out of the casings first. Use the seasoned flour to coat the meatballs.

(Mix the ground meat and sausage meat together if you're using both.)

2. Fry the meatballs, the zucchini, and the chopped onions pieces
   in a couple of tablespoons of olive oil in a large pan or wok for
   a few minutes, then add the chopped tomatoes. Bring to a
   boil and stir in the cayenne pepper and whatever other spices
   or herbs you want to use.
3. Tear the spinach leaves up and add to the sauce, followed by
   the noodles.
4. Simmer gently for a couple of minutes until the noodles are
   just soft. Adjust the seasoning and serve.

## Bacon Cakes

SERVES 4
6 strips bacon
1 onion, very finely chopped
2 medium potatoes
2 tablespoons self-rising flour
Salt and pepper
2 eggs
Oil

1. Snip the bacon into tiny pieces, finely chop the onion, peel,
   wash, rinse, and grate the potatoes, and put everything in a
   mixing bowl.
2. Stir the flour and seasoning into the mixture, followed by the
   eggs, and beat it all together.
3. Warm the oil in a large frying pan and put spoonfuls of the
   mixture into the hot oil, flatten them slightly, and cook for a

few minutes, turning once, until the bacon cakes are crisp and brown.

4. Keep warm in the oven or under the broiler (on low) and serve with baked beans.

## One-Step Pasta

Use the smallest dried pasta shapes for extra speed; the ones made especially for kids are ideal, although they tend to be more expensive. Fresh pasta requires even less cooking time—about 3 minutes—in which case, put the frankfurters in first.

SERVES 4–6
Dried pasta shapes (about one handful per person)
10 skinny frankfurters, sliced
A handful of frozen whole kernel corn
A handful of sugar snap peas
Olive oil or butter
Cherry tomatoes
Grated cheese

1. Put the pasta into boiling salted water.
2. After about 5 minutes add the sliced frankfurters and corn.
3. Put the sugar snap peas in for the last 2 minutes.
4. When the pasta is cooked, strain the whole lot together. Stir in a very little olive oil or butter and serve with cherry tomatoes and grated cheese.

## Instant Corned Beef Hash

Traditionally made with leftover boiled potatoes, a very unorthodox version of corned beef hash can be made with instant mashed potatoes. (You may not have stooped this low before, but once you've got more than one child to transport from A to B in record time every night—or you're just too tired to care— you will, I assure you.)

If you're making this for more than four people, especially older kids and adults, you'll need to double up the quantities below.

SERVES 4
1 can corned beef
1 large onion
Oil
Instant mashed potato made with milk and water

1. Cut the corned beef into chunks and peel and thinly slice the onion.
2. Warm enough oil to just cover the bottom of a large frying pan. Fry the corned beef and onion in the hot oil for a few minutes until brown, while you make the instant mashed potato according to the instructions on the package.
3. Add the potato to the pan, turning it over every few seconds until it's as crisp and brown as you want it to be.
4. Serve with baked beans.

### Shrimp & Egg Pie

For a deluxe version of Shrimp & Egg Pie, make shortcrust pastry in the usual way with about ½ pound (225 g) of all-purpose flour, then grease and line a deep-sided pie dish (or a 7-inch or 8-inch cake pan) and layer the ingredients, starting and finishing with grated cheese and adding beaten egg twice, once about halfway up the pie and again just before the final layer of cheese.

The quick-fix Shrimp & Egg Pie is equally good hot or cold and should serve four adults, but it's worth noting that you can make two pies as easily as one; all you need to do is buy an extra ready-made pie crust dough and double up the ingredients below.

Add lemon juice, salt, black pepper, and chives or basil, as you like.

MAKES 1 PIE

1 pie crust made from rolled ready-made pastry, such as Pillsbury
1 tomato
A handful of spinach
1 small package frozen shrimp, defrosted
1 egg
Dash of milk
Grated cheese

1. Preheat oven to 375°F (190°C). Line a 7-inch pie dish with the pastry.
2. Wash and cut the tomato into half slices. Tear or shred the spinach and rinse the shrimp.
3. Beat the egg, adding a dash of milk, then mix with the rest of the ingredients, saving some of the cheese for the top of the pie.
4. Pour the filling into the crust, spreading it out as evenly as possible, and sprinkle with the remaining cheese.
5. Bake for about 15 minutes, until the top is a light golden brown.

### Fish Stick Pie

Fish sticks (2–4 per person, depending on size of person)
Tomatoes
Spinach
Grating cheese

1. Place the fish sticks side by side in batches of 2–4 and cook as directed on the package.
2. Wash and slice the tomatoes, shred the spinach, and grate the cheese.
3. Turn the fish sticks over and broil on the second side for 2 minutes; no longer.
4. Cover each batch of fish sticks with a layer of spinach and top with the slices of tomato and cheese; broil for a few more minutes and serve.

Note: *Oven fries don't take longer than half an hour, so put some on before you start if you've got another five or ten minutes to spare.*

## Smoked Salmon and Tagliatelli

For extra speed use fresh tagliatelle, but be careful not to over-cook before you return it to the pan with the smoked salmon and crème fraîche. (You could also add a few shrimp at the same time if you like.)

Best served with salad (cucumber, watercress, or baby leaf spinach and avocado) or green vegetables (French beans, snow peas, or sugar snap peas).

SERVES 4–6
3–4 slices of smoked salmon
Baby plum or cherry tomatoes
Balsamic vinegar
Tagliatelle (one generous handful per person)
4 tablespoons crème fraîche
Parsley, chopped

1. Slice the smoked salmon quite thinly, halve the tomatoes, and sprinkle the tomatoes with balsamic vinegar.

2. Prepare a salad or whichever green vegetables you want to serve, according to the instructions on the package—a couple of minutes in the microwave should be all they need.

3. Simmer the tagliatelle in boiling water until it's *just done*, then strain through a colander.

4. Soften the crème fraîche in the still-warm pan over the lowest heat, then return the pasta to the saucepan with the smoked salmon, crème fraîche, and parsley.

5. Stir well and gently warm through for a couple of minutes before serving with the tomatoes and vegetables.

### Fastest-Ever Fish Cakes

MAKES 6
1 large can red or pink salmon (about 14.75 ounces/418 g)
2 eggs, beaten
2 tablespoons lemon juice
Salt and pepper
½ cup (60 g) self-rising flour
Parsley, chopped
Oil

1. Drain the can of salmon and mash the fish in a bowl with a fork. (Pick out any extra big bits of skin but leave the bones in and crush them up with the fish.)

2. Add the beaten eggs, lemon juice, seasoning, sifted flour, and parsley and mix well.

3. Warm enough oil in a large frying pan to cover the bottom of the pan and drop spoonfuls of the mixture into the hot oil, pressing gently into a cake shape with the spatula and turning once. Serve with lemon wedges and a salad.

# THINGS ON TOAST

*Just in case you need reminding, the following things are all brilliant on toast and help transform a couple of slices of bread into a makeshift meal . . .*

BAKED BEANS Spread the toast with butter first and top the beans with grated cheese. (English baked beans are made with tomato sauce. Heinz brand import is widely available in the U.S., or substitute Campbell's Pork and Beans in Tomato Sauce.)

OILY FISH Canned sardines or mackerel in tomato sauce are both good sources of those omega-3 fatty acids that we're always hearing about. Toast the bread on one side, turn it over and top with the mashed-up fish; no need for butter, but especially good with lashings of tomato ketchup.

TUNA AND CHEESE MELT Tuna mixed with grated cheese; toast and serve as above.

CHEESE Topped and broiled with thinly sliced tomato, or on its own with a dash of Worcestershire sauce, or a spoonful of sweet pickle or chutney.

EGGS Scrambled or poached, with sliced ham or leftover cold sausages.

ALSO TRY . . .
Chicken and Leek Casserole (page 237).
Omelettes (page 239).
Sweet & Sour Chicken (page 54).

"Soup and fish explain half the emotions of human life."

—Sydney Smith

# 5
# The joy of soup

*There's nothing to beat good old-fashioned soup made with fresh ingredients when it comes to availability, versatility, and the art of saving money on your supermarket shopping.*

If you want to lose weight sensibly and painlessly without reducing your energy levels, you could do a lot worse than including plenty of homemade soups in your diet. All soups freeze well and can be stored in large and small amounts; for family dinners, or for taking to work and reheating in the microwave—very handy when you want to avoid the temptations of the deli or sandwich bar.

Make soup more appealing to children by adding croutons, grated cheese, and pasta shapes, or give them a bit less soup (a little goes a long way in any case) with a hot dog or toasted sandwich on the side.

You can't go far wrong with soup whatever you do, so use these recipes as a guideline and make the rest up as you go along.

### Tips

To thicken soup, whisk in a couple of tablespoons of instant mash potato granules, while the soup is still warm. Almost as outrageous as a celebrity chef using Knorr stock cubes, but there it is.

Unless otherwise specified in the recipe, add the herbs and spices mixed with the stock for even distribution.

Add a spoonful of Marmite or Vegemite to larger amounts of stock, instead of a second stock cube.

Use alternative herbs and spices if you like, but don't leave them out altogether; they do make a difference. (Buy bouquet garni already made up in little tea bags to save time.)

For creamed soups, pour cream over the surface in a circular movement, straight from the carton, or create a marbled effect by zigzagging a knife or the edge of a metal spoon through the trail of cream.

## Orange Squash Soup

Butter
Sunflower oil
1 butternut squash (any size)
1 pound (500 g) carrots
1 large onion
1 clove garlic, crushed
1 small orange
Ground ginger
Ground coriander
Salt and white pepper
3 cups (750 ml) chicken or vegetable stock

1. Melt the butter in the oil in a large saucepan while you peel the butternut squash (removing the seeds and pithy inside completely) and scrape the carrots.
2. Roughly chop the squash, carrots, and onion, put them in the pan with the crushed garlic and cook to soften over low heat for a few minutes.
3. Add the zest of half the orange to the saucepan with the ginger, coriander, salt, and pepper.
4. Cut the orange into quarters and make sure to remove the seeds. Give each quarter a little squeeze as you add it to the

pan, then pour over the chicken or vegetable stock and give it a good stir.

5. Bring to a boil, cover with a lid, then reduce the heat and simmer gently for about 30 minutes.
6. Remove the orange quarters and discard.
7. Blend the soup and add additional salt and pepper to taste.

## Celery Soup

There's an even quicker way to make this soup; just put the raw ingredients with the seasoning, milk, and wine in the food processor, blend until smooth (one minute, maximum), then heat it up in a large saucepan.

Butter
Sunflower oil
1 head celery, leaves left on
1 large onion
1 clove garlic, crushed
2 tablespoons all-purpose flour
2 cups (500 ml) chicken or vegetable stock
Celery salt or salt and white pepper
1 great big glug of white wine (about half a glass)
½ cups (125 ml) milk

1. Melt the butter in the oil in a large saucepan.
2. Wash and chop the celery and onion and cook gently over a low heat for a few minutes with the crushed garlic until softened.
3. Stir in the flour and cook for another minute.
4. Add the chicken or vegetable stock with the seasoning. Bring to a boil, then reduce the heat, add the wine and milk, and simmer gently for up to 30 minutes.

5. Blend the soup in batches if necessary. Taste and adjust the seasoning.

## Watercress Soup

Another good one for speed and simplicity (not to mention a healthy dose of iron), is watercress soup, which also doubles as a great sauce to use with any white fish or salmon.

Butter
1 onion, chopped
1 clove garlic, crushed
Parsley, chopped
1 or 2 bags of watercress (or a couple of large bunches) depending on size
2 tablespoons all-purpose flour
2 cups (500 ml) chicken or vegetable stock
½ cup (125 ml) milk
Salt and pepper
Light cream

1. Melt the butter in a large saucepan, add the onion along with the garlic and parsley and cook gently for a few minutes until the onion is soft.
2. Add the watercress, cover the pan with a lid, and cook for another few minutes.
3. Stir in the flour and keep stirring for another minute, then remove the pan from the heat and add the stock and milk. Season with salt and pepper.
4. Bring the soup to a boil, stirring occasionally, then reduce the heat, and simmer for another 5 minutes.
5. Blend the soup in batches if necessary.

6. To serve add a swirl of cream to each individual bowl and garnish with sprigs of watercress, or sprinkle more parsley on top.

## Stinging Nettle Soup

I've always liked the idea of making soup with nettles. There's something very appealing about a type of leaf that's plentiful, accessible, full of vitamins and minerals, and—until someone decides to market stinging nettles as the latest, must-have ingredient—they're FREE!

This recipe is more or less the same as the one for watercress soup (above) and, not surprisingly, the end result also looks and tastes very similar. The difference is you need a pair of rubber gloves to make this soup; the nettles don't lose their sting until they're cooked and, as you'd expect, they also need to be washed more carefully.

Pick only the top two or three inches of the youngest, brightest green nettles you can find, and don't worry too much about the quantity; as a rough guide, the equivalent of a medium-sized bag of watercress or spinach is just fine.

Nettles
Butter
1 onion
2 cloves garlic
1 tablespoon malt vinegar
2 cups (500 ml) chicken stock (made from stock cubes)
½ cup (125 ml) milk
1 teaspoon nutmeg
2 heaping tablespoons all-purpose flour
2 teaspoons dried parsley
Salt and pepper

1. Wearing rubber gloves, plunge the nettles into a bowl of cold water with lots of salt, and fish them out a few at a time to wash thoroughly in another bowl of cold water, or under cold running water, until you're sure they're clean. (Remove any big, tough stems if there are any, otherwise the leaves can stay attached to the stems.)

2. Warm some butter in a large saucepan while you peel and chop the onion and crush the garlic, then add them to the pan and cook gently for a few minutes until the onion has softened.

3. Squeeze any excess water from the nettles (still wearing the rubber gloves) and add them to the pan with a spoonful of vinegar. Cover the pan with a lid and simmer gently for about 5 minutes, then add the chicken stock, milk, and nutmeg.

4. Stir well and bring the soup to a boil while you mash the flour, butter, and the dried parsley together in a cup or bowl, until smooth.

5. As soon as the nettle soup has started to boil, reduce the heat, add the parsley, butter and flour mixture, and stir until dissolved, then let it simmer gently for about 5 minutes. Season with salt and pepper.

6. Blend the soup in batches if necessary. Garnish each serving with a fresh sprig of nettle—Only joking!

## Sweet Potato Soup

2 sweet potatoes

2–3 carrots

1 onion

4 cups (1 liter) chicken or vegetable stock (made from 2 stock cubes)

1 tablespoon butter

3–4 strips bacon
1 tablespoon all-purpose flour
Salt and pepper

1. Peel and chop the vegetables and make the stock.
2. Melt the butter in a large pan and pop the bacon in for a couple of minutes on its own, then add the vegetables and fry for 5 minutes more.
3. Add the flour and cook for 1 minute.
4. Stir in the stock, bring to a boil. Reduce the heat, cover with a lid, and simmer for about 30 minutes, or until all the vegetables are soft. Season with salt and pepper.
5. Allow to cool for a few minutes, then blend the soup in batches if necessary. Taste and adjust the seasoning.

## Lentil and Vegetable Soup

There's no end to what you can do with lentils and vegetables; use red or yellow lentils if you want to avoid soaking the lentils in advance, otherwise brown and green lentils or chickpeas will do.

Oil
1 onion, chopped
2 cloves garlic, crushed
1 cup (about 200 g) red lentils
2 small potatoes, peeled and diced
½ small rutabaga, peeled and diced
2–3 carrots, scraped and chopped
1 small parsnip, scraped and chopped
2–3 celery stalks, finely chopped
Salt and pepper

4 cups (1 liter) vegetable stock (made from 2 stock cubes)
Parsley, chopped

OPTIONAL
1 level teaspoon curry powder

1. Warm the oil in a very large saucepan and gently fry the onion and garlic until the onion is soft.
2. Add the lentils and cook for 1 minute.
3. Add the rest of the vegetables and salt and pepper (and optional curry) and cook over low heat for another 5 minutes or so.
4. Add the stock, bring to a boil, reduce the heat, and simmer for 20–30 minutes until the vegetables are soft.
5. Blend the soup in batches if necessary. Taste and adjust the seasoning, and serve garnished with parsley.

## Spicy Bean Soup

High in fiber, low in fat, and cheaper than fries—use fresh beans if you like, but canned ones are normally just as good.

This soup isn't blended at the end, so slice or dice the vegetables finely, the way you want them to look in the finished soup.

Oil
4 slices back bacon, rind and fat removed, or Irish bacon
2 celery stalks, finely chopped
2 carrots, finely chopped
2 zucchini, finely chopped
1 onion, finely chopped
2 cloves garlic, crushed
4 cups (1 liter) beef, lamb, or pork stock

1 level teaspoon curry powder or ground cumin
½ teaspoon mixed spice
2 bay leaves
Worcestershire sauce
Any 2 different cans of beans from the following list: borlotti
    beans, butter beans, broad beans, canellini beans, kidney
    beans, or chickpeas
2–3 tablespoons instant mashed potato granules

1.  Heat the oil in a very large pan, snip the bacon into small
    pieces, and fry until crisp and golden while you prepare the
    vegetables.
2.  Add the finely chopped celery, carrots, zucchini, onion, and
    garlic and fry for another 10 minutes until everything has
    softened.
3.  Add the stock with the spices, bay leaves, and Worcestershire
    sauce mixed in and simmer for 15–20 minutes.
4.  Drain the cans of beans in a colander, add them to the soup,
    and simmer for another 5 minutes.
5.  To finish: Remove the bay leaf. Sprinkle the instant mashed
    potato granules into the soup, and whisk with a small hand
    whisk or a fork until dissolved.

## Tomato & Red Lentil Soup

This can be thinned down and used as the sauce for a pasta bake
(*see Salmon & Tomato Bake, page 247*).

It goes without saying that you can always use fresh ingredients
instead of canned if you want to, so if you're using fresh tomatoes
for this, put them in a pan of very hot water for a minute, then
scoop them out with a slotted spoon; the skin should peel away
easily and they're ready to use.

2 onions
4 strips bacon
1 cup (about 200 g) red lentils
Butter
Olive oil
2–3 cans chopped or plum tomatoes (about 14.5 ounces/411 g
   each) or 2 lbs (1 kg) fresh tomatoes
5 cups (1.25 liters) chicken stock (made from 2 stock cubes)
1 teaspoon brown sugar
Dried basil
Salt and pepper

1. Roughly chop the onions, snip the bacon into pieces, and wash
   the lentils thoroughly in a sieve or colander.
2. Melt a little butter with some olive oil in a large saucepan and
   fry the onion and bacon for a few minutes until golden.
3. Add the lentils to the pan, followed by the tomatoes, stock,
   sugar, and seasonings, and stir well.
4. Bring to the boil and simmer gently for about 30 minutes.
5. Blend the soup in batches if necessary. Adjust the seasoning
   and thin the soup down with a little more stock, milk, or
   tomato juice, according to taste.

## Minestrone

Use whichever beans you like; borlotti, cannellini, kidney beans,
chickpeas, or mixed beans.

Olive oil
4–6 strips bacon
1 onion, diced
2 celery stalks, diced

2 zucchini, diced
2 carrots diced
1 small green and 1 red pepper, diced
2 cloves garlic, crushed
1 standard can chopped tomatoes (about 14.5 ounces/411 g)
5 cups (1.25 liters) chicken stock (made from 2 stock cubes)
Dried oregano or mixed Italian seasoning
Dried basil
1 teaspoon light brown sugar
4 ounces (100 g) or ½ cup small pasta shapes, such as farfalline
1 can beans (about 14.5 ounces/411 g)
Black pepper
Tomato paste (optional)
Croutons
Parmesan, or other grated cheese

1. Warm a little oil in a very large saucepan and fry the bacon and onion until crisp and golden while you prepare the rest of the vegetables. (Don't add anything else to the pan too soon or you'll never get the bacon crisp.)
2. Add the celery, zucchini, carrots, peppers, and garlic, followed by the chopped tomatoes and the chicken stock mixed with the herbs and sugar.
3. Stir well, bring to the boil, and simmer gently for about 10 minutes.
4. Add the pasta and the canned beans and simmer for another 15–20 minutes, until the vegetables and pasta are just soft.
5. Season to taste, add a little tomato paste if you like, and serve with croutons and Parmesan, or any other grated cheese.

## Smoked Mackerel Chowder

Don't worry too much about the size and weight of the fish, or the number of fillets in the packet; the chowder will turn out okay however much fish you use.

Potatoes (about 4 medium or 6 small)
1 onion
2 leeks
Butter
Oil
1 tablespoon all-purpose flour
2 serving spoons frozen whole kernel corn (about 4 tablespoons)
3 cups (750 ml) milk (whole or 2 percent skimmed)
½ cup (125 ml) light cream
1 package smoked mackerel fillets
Dried parsley (about 2 teaspoons)

1. Peel the potatoes and chop into small chunks; wash and finely chop the onion and leeks.
2. Melt butter and oil in a large saucepan and gently brown the potatoes for a few minutes. Add the onion and leeks and fry for a few more minutes until the onion has softened, then stir in the flour and cook for another minute.
3. Add the frozen corn, pour in the milk with the cream, and bring to a boil while you remove the skin from the mackerel and flake the fish, making sure there aren't any bones.
4. Reduce the heat as soon as the milk and cream reach a boil, then add the mackerel to the pan with parsley to taste. Stir well and let simmer for about 20 minutes, or until the potatoes are just soft.
5. If you want to thicken the chowder at the end of the cook-

ing, add ½ teaspoon of cornstarch to another 2 tablespoons cream. For a thinner consistency, just add more milk.

## MEAT SOUPS

Soups in which meat is the main ingredient naturally take longer to cook, but the preparation is still straightforward—and once the soup is cooking you can go off and do something else.

### Borscht

I hated beets as a child, and even though they're never going to be one of my favorite vegetables (I still can't stand them pickled in vinegar), I do like borscht. It probably helps that I put less beet and more beef in mine than in some of the other recipes I've seen, so if you also think you hate beets, give borscht a try; you might be pleasantly surprised.

About 2 pounds (1 kg) stewing or braising steak
1 onion
A few cloves
1 carrot
1–2 celery stalks
Bouquet garni
2 raw beets
½ small white cabbage
1 standard can chopped tomatoes (about 14.5 ounces/411 g)
Tomato paste
2 teaspoons brown sugar
2 bay leaves
Butter mixed with all-purpose flour (optional)
1 small carton sour cream

1. Trim any fat off the meat and cut it into small, even pieces, then put in a large saucepan with 4 cups (1 liter) of fresh, cold water.
2. Peel the onion, leaving it whole, and stick a few cloves into it.
3. Wash the carrot and celery stalks; leave them whole or cut them in half so they're easier to fish out of the pan later on.
4. Put the onion, carrot, celery, and bouquet garni into the pan with the meat over high heat and bring to the boil.
5. When the water is boiling, reduce the heat, skim the scum off the top with a slotted spoon, cover with a lid, and leave the soup to simmer very gently for about 30 minutes.
6. Meanwhile, peel and cut the beets into matchstick-sized pieces and finely shred the cabbage.
7. When the meat is *almost* tender, remove and discard the carrots, onion, celery, and bouquet garni, and use a cup or ladle to remove about one-fourth of the liquid.
8. Add the beets, cabbage, and the rest of the ingredients: the tomatoes, tomato paste, sugar, and bay leaves and simmer very gently for about 1 hour, until the beef is very tender.
9. When the soup is ready, remove the bay leaves and discard. If you want the soup to be a bit less liquid, thicken it with a tablespoon of butter mixed with 1 tablespoon all-purpose flour.
10. To finish, add sour cream to the Borscht. Serve with Soda Bread (page 204).

## Chicken Soup

Use a chicken carcass to make the stock for chicken soup; it's a lot less hassle than you might think. It doesn't matter whether you use the whole cooked chicken or just the remains from a roast chicken, but ideally you should have at least one-third of the meat left for the soup.

This soup is half-blended, so cut the vegetables for the finished soup into smaller pieces than you would for the stock.

THE STOCK
Chicken carcass
2 bay leaves
4 black peppercorns
1 onion
2 carrots
2 stalks celery
3–4 pints (2 liters) fresh, cold water

THE SOUP
3 medium potatoes
2–3 carrots
2–3 celery stalks
1 onion
Oil
Butter
5⅛ cups (1.2 liters) fresh chicken stock
1 bouquet garni
1 small/medium organic chicken, cooked
Salt and pepper
½ cup (125 ml) light cream

OPTIONAL
Dried thyme or tarragon

FOR THE STOCK
1. Remove the skin and as much meat as you can from the cooked chicken; discard the skin, cut into small pieces, and set the meat aside.

2. Put the chicken carcass in a very large pot with the bay leaves, peppercorns, and the onion, carrots, and celery; all washed and roughly chopped. Cover with fresh, cold water.
3. Bring to the boil, then reduce the heat and simmer gently for up to 4 hours, or longer if you have time, but ideally no less than 2 hours.
4. When the stock is done, remove the chicken carcass, vegetables, and bay leaves and give the stock a good stir with a slotted spoon to make sure it's clear. *Note: If you think you've got a lot more stock than you want for the quantity of soup you're making, take out what you don't need now and keep it in the fridge for a couple of days, or freeze it for up to 3 months.*

FOR THE SOUP
1. Cut the potatoes, carrots, celery, and onion into small pieces and fry them in oil or butter (or a bit of both) for a few minutes, in a very large saucepan.
2. Add the stock with the optional herbs and the bouquet garni *(see Notes, page 112)*, bring to the boil, reduce the heat, and simmer gently for about 30 minutes, or until the vegetables are tender but not mushy.
3. Remove the bouquet garni and blend half of the soup. Mix the remainder of the soup with the blended half and add the chicken pieces. Warm the soup thoroughly, season with salt and pepper, and add the cream at the end.

Note: *If you're making the soup for later, rather than serve immediately it straightaway, allow the soup to cool before adding the chicken pieces.*

## Scotch Broth

The first and, until recently, the last time I made Scotch Broth was at school, which, thinking about it now, must be an indication of two things; one, how times have changed, and two, how simple this must be if a thirteen-year-old could make it. (It was perfectly edible as well; we ate what I made at home.)

I can't for the life of me think why I haven't made it before now, not least because it's great to be able to buy cheaper cuts of meat, knowing all it takes is a little time and gentle cooking to make it as tender and delicious as the more expensive ones.

I used 1 ½ pounds (725 g) of neck fillet (if you have a butcher, ask for scrag end of lamb) or if you prefer, use a similar amount of beef stewing steak.

1–2 pounds (500 g–1 kg) meat
2–3 carrots
2 leeks
½ small rutabaga, or 2–3 white turnips, depending on size
2 onions
5–6 tablespoons pearl barley
Parsley, chopped
2 lamb or beef stock cubes
Salt and pepper

1. Cut up the meat with kitchen scissors; put the pieces in a large saucepan with enough cold water to cover (about 5 cups, 1.5 liters) and simmer, covered, for 1 ½ hours. Skim the fat off the surface once or twice.
2. Wash, peel, and dice the vegetables. 10–15 minutes before the end of the cooking time.
3. Put the barley into a small saucepan with just enough cold water to cover. Boil for a few minutes, then strain through a sieve and rinse under the cold running water. (You don't have to blanch the barley this way, but it helps to prevent a scum forming on the finished soup.)

4. Add the barley, vegetables, parsley, and stock cubes to the pan with the meat and simmer very gently for about 30 minutes until the vegetables and barley are just soft. Season to taste with salt and pepper.
5. Serve the broth, adding as much of the liquid from the pan as you wish.

# CHILLED SOUPS

## Cool Cucumber Soup

A cool soup for a hot summer's day—be sure to add to touch of green with a sprinkling of chopped fresh mint leaves or dill fronds.

2 large cucumbers
1 small onion
Butter
1 tablespoon all-purpose flour
2 cups (500 ml) warm milk
1 cup (250 ml) chicken stock (made with 1 stock cube)
½ teaspoon ground nutmeg
Salt and pepper
⅔ cup (150 ml) light cream
Fresh mint or dill fronds chopped

1. Peel and halve the cucumbers and scoop out the seedy bit in the middle. Chop the cucumbers into chunks and peel and chop the onion.
2. Melt some butter in a large saucepan, fry the cucumber and onion for a few minutes, then add the flour and cook for another minute, stirring all the time.

3. Meanwhile, warm the milk in a separate saucepan and make 1 cup (250 ml) of stock with 1 stock cube in a measuring cup, adding the nutmeg and seasoning to the hot stock.

4. Remove the pan with the vegetables from the heat and gradually pour in the stock and warm milk, stirring continuously.

5. Bring the soup to the boil, still stirring, then reduce the heat and simmer gently for about 20 minutes.

6. Allow the soup to cool for a few minutes then puree in a blender or food processor in batches if necessary. Taste and adjust the seasoning.

7. Chill the soup in the fridge for at least 2 hours; serve with a swirl of cream and a sprinkling of mint or dill fronds.

## Hot or Cold Leek & Potato Soup

This is, basically, a recipe for Vichyssoise, a classic elegant, cold soup, but it's also very good hot, so you decide.

1 pound (450 g) potatoes
1 pound (450 g) leeks (white part only)
1 medium onion
Butter
Oil
1 clove garlic, crushed
3 cups (750 ml) chicken stock
Salt and pepper
⅔ cup (150 ml) light cream
Chives, chopped

1. Peel the potatoes, rinse well, and cut into small chunks. Remove the green part of the leeks and the root end. Wash the

white of the leeks throughly and slice crosswise. Chop the onion.

2. Warm butter and oil in a large saucepan, add the crushed garlic and the vegetables, then cover the pan with a lid and cook gently for a few minutes.

3. Pour in the stock, season with salt and pepper, and bring to the boil. Reduce the heat and simmer gently for 20–30 minutes until the vegetables are just soft.

4. Allow the soup to cool for a few minutes, then blend thoroughly in batches if necessary, until the soup is very smooth. Taste and adjust the seasoning, then either chill the soup in the fridge for a couple of hours, or reheat when ready to use. Hot or cold, finish the soup with cream and a sprinkling of chives.

"Part of the secret of success in life is to eat what you like and let the food fight it out inside."

—Mark Twain

# 6
# Join the pudding club

*Dessert as an everyday thing fell out of fashion years ago, which is hardly surprising when we're obsessed with healthy eating, more women than ever are out at work and you can already buy everything from profiteroles to pavlova in the supermarket.*

But it can't be right that the nation who gave the world spotted dick and treacle tart (not to mention apple pie, which is English whatever they think in America) should give up homemade desserts altogether and settle for a gloomy future of frozen lemon meringue pie, so if you think you haven't got time for desserts, think again. Plenty of desserts take only a minimal amount of time and effort, and there's nothing like the promise of something sweet for getting kids to dutifully eat more of the things you really want them to have first.

Having said that, desserts or puddings, as we British call them, aren't necessarily an unhealthy option either, especially when they contain a lot of fruit, and as a truly satisfying comfort food they do a lot less damage to your diet than a family-sized bar of chocolate or a bag of doughnuts.

Try and make desserts a part of your life; even once a week is better than never. Your family and friends will love you for it.

## Tips

Pour evaporated milk (preferably Carnation) over fresh and canned fruit puddings as a cheap and easy alternative to cream or custard.

Buy golden syrup and maple syrup in plastic bottles for easy squeezing.

Cool Jell-O quickly by adding slightly less cold water to the melted gelatin and popping in 2 or 3 ice cubes.

Make sour cream by adding 1 tablespoon of lemon juice to ⅔ cup (150 ml) of light cream.

Make chocolate custard simply by mixing 1 ounce (25 g) of chocolate into warm custard, ready-made or instant; or melt the chocolate in the microwave first and stir it in.

## Pastry

A basic shortcrust pastry is all you'll ever need for most pies and flans; add 1 level tablespoon of superfine granulated or confectioners' sugar to make it slightly sweeter. The quantities given below make enough pastry to line a shallow, loose-bottomed 8-inch (15cm) tart pan or pie dish.

### SHORTCRUST PASTRY
1¼ cups (150 g) all-purpose flour
5½ tablespoons (75 g) butter or margarine
1 heaping tablespoon superfine granulated sugar (or confectioners' sugar)
4 tablespoons cold water

1. Preheat oven to 350°F (180°C). Sift the flour into a very large mixing bowl and rub in the butter or margarine in small pieces until the mixture resembles fine bread crumbs.
2. Stir in the sugar, make a well in the center, then add the water, gradually incorporating the flour by pinching the mixture together with the fingers of one hand. Knead the pas-

try inside the bowl for a minute to make a firm, smooth dough.

3. Wrap the dough in aluminium foil or a double layer of plastic wrap and chill in the fridge for half an hour before rolling.

4. Turn the dough out onto a lightly floured surface and roll it out to fit the lightly greased tart pan, or pie dish.

5. Prick the pastry with a fork several times before adding the filling. If the pastry case is to be baked "blind"—on its own so the filling can be added when the pastry is cold—cover it with a circle of parchment paper and then weigh the paper down with a handful of dried beans, lentils, or rice.

6. Bake for 10–15 minutes. (Remove the dried beans and parchment paper and return to the oven for a further 5 minutes to crisp the pastry.)

# CHEESECAKE

*If you also have an irrational fear of recipes containing gelatin, these are the cheesecakes for you . . .*

### Cherry Cheesecake

If you can't find the exact quantities of cherries and cream cheese mentioned here, get the nearest sizes up and if the cherries aren't pitted, remove the stones yourself by making a little cut down one side of the fruit with a sharp knife and gently squeezing out the stone.

An even easier option is to buy a can of cherry pie filling, mix half with the beaten cream cheese, and spread the remainder over the top of the cheesecake, thinning it with a little fruit juice first, if need be.

SERVES 4–6
THE COOKIE BASE
½ stick (4 tablespoons) (56 g) butter
8 large English digestive biscuits or graham crackers, crushed
by hand

THE CHEESECAKE
1 can black cherries in heavy syrup (about 15 ounces/425 g)
1 heaping tablespoon sugar (white or light brown)
2 tablespoons Amaretto or similar liqueur
1 rounded tablespoon cornstarch
8 ounces (227 g) softened cream cheese

1. Lightly grease a 6- to 7-inch (12 cm) springform cake pan.
2. Make the cookie base by melting the butter in a saucepan and
   adding the crushed crumbs. (You can make the crumbs in a
   food processor but it only takes a minute to crush the biscuits
   or graham crackers up in a large bowl using your thumbs or a
   china mug.)
3. Press the crumb mixture into the prepared cake pan and chill
   in the fridge for about 30 minutes.
4. Separate the cherries from the syrup, reserving the syrup, and
   cut the cherries in half.
5. Pour the syrup into a saucepan with the sugar and liqueur, add
   the cornstarch and stir quickly and constantly over a medium
   heat for a few minutes until the syrup becomes thick and
   smooth, like a gel.
6. Remove the pan from the heat, add the cherries, and mix together.
7. To make the filling, beat the cream cheese in a bowl until
   smooth (this only takes a few seconds with a wooden spoon),

then add half the cherries and blend with the beaten cream cheese.

8.  Spread the filling over the chilled base and top with the remainder of the cherries.
9.  Chill for at least an hour and serve with light cream.

## Lemon Cheesecake

This cheesecake works well with a pastry or a cookie base (use a ready-made graham cracker crust if you don't have time to make one) and, needless to say, you can use any flavor Jell-O with a mixture of whatever canned and fresh fruit you like.

SERVES 4–6
½ stick (4 tablespoons) (56 g) butter
8 large English digestive biscuits or graham crackers, crushed
1 small package lemon Jell-O
8 ounces (227 g) softened cream cheese
2 crème fraîche

TO DECORATE
Kiwifruit
Strawberries
Canned peaches

1.  Lightly grease a 6- to 7-inch (12 cm) springform cake pan.
2.  Make the cookie base by melting the butter in a saucepan and adding the crushed crumbs. (You can make the crumbs in a food processor, but it takes only a minute to crush the biscuits or graham crackers up in a large bowl using your thumbs or a china mug.)

3. Put the Jell-O in a large measuring cup with 1 cup (250 ml) of boiling water and stir for a few minutes until dissolved. *Don't top up with cold water in the usual way;* instead add 2 or 3 ice cubes to cool the Jell-O down quickly, then leave it to stand for 20–30 minutes.
4. Put the cream cheese in a large mixing bowl with the cool Jell-O and crème fraîche and beat it all together with an electric hand mixer for half a minute until smooth.
5. Spread the filling evenly over the cookie base and leave to set in the fridge for at least an hour.
6. Decorate the top of the cheesecake with thin slices of strawberry, kiwifruit, and canned peaches—or whatever else you fancy.

## Cheshire Tart

Cheshire Tart is actually a baked cheesecake. And still not a gelatin leaf in sight.

SERVES 4–6
THE COOKIE BASE
8 large English digestive biscuits, or graham crackers, crushed
4 English ginger biscuits, or ginger cookies
5½ tablespoons (75 g) butter, melted
½ teaspoon ground ginger
1 tablespoon golden syrup

THE FILLING
3 eggs, separated
1¼ cups (100 g) Cheshire or cheddar cheese, finely grated
8 ounces (227 g) softened cream cheese

2 tablespoons plain natural yogurt or crème fraîche
2 teaspoons sugar
2 tablespoons lemon juice

1.  Preheat oven to 300°F (150°C). Make the cookie base in the usual way (*see page 136*); crushing the cookies by hand, then mixing thoroughly with the melted butter, ginger, and golden syrup.
2.  Lightly grease and line a 6- to 7-inch (12 cm) springform pan with parchment paper. Press the crumb mixture into the lined pan.
3.  Separate the eggs into two large mixing bowls and add the grated cheese, cream cheese, yogurt or crème fraîche, sugar, and lemon juice to the bowl with the egg yolks.
4.  First whisk the egg whites, with an electric hand mixer, until they stand up in peaks and all the bubbles have disappeared; then whisk together the ingredients in the second bowl.
5.  Gently fold the egg whites into the cheese mixture until the ingredients are combined, then pour the mixture onto the cookie base. Bake for 45 minutes to an hour, until the top is firm and set and slightly golden.
6.  Allow the cheesecake to cool in the pan for about an hour, then run a sharp knife around the edge and carefully remove it from the pan.
7.  Dust the top of the cheesecake with confectioners' sugar, and serve with fresh fruit and light cream.

## Baked Apples

You could say baked apples are a quick-fix dessert; they take no more than five minutes to prepare and you can put them in the oven as you're taking the main course out so they're ready to eat straight after dinner. (They also make a nice change for a weekend breakfast with yogurt and honey or crème fraîche.)

If you haven't got an apple corer, remove the center of the apples by putting them on a hard, flat surface and pushing a sharp knife through each one four times in a square shape around the stem, making sure you go right to the bottom every time; then turn the apple over and repeat the process from the other end. Now use your thumb to push the core out.

(Stick two or three whole cloves into the apple for extra flavor and remove after cooking.)

1 large baking apple per person with:
 golden raisins or mixed fruit with mixed spice and brown
 sugar or chopped dried apricots with golden syrup and
 cinnamon or dried cranberries and superfine granulated
 sugar
Cream, crème fraîche, evaporated milk, or custard for serving

1. Preheat oven to 350°F (180°C). Wash the apples, remove the cores, and score a line all the way around each apple, halfway down and about ½ inch (1 cm) deep.
2. Mix the fruit with the sugar and spices in a small bowl.
3. Place the apples in an ovenproof dish and stuff with as much of the fruit as you can get in the middle of each apple, scattering whatever's left over around the base.
4. Cover loosely with aluminium foil and bake for about 40 minutes, or until the apples are just soft. Remove the cloves. Serve with cream, crème fraîche, or custard sauce.

## Rhubarb Crumble

Crumbles are the perfect alternative to pies, because you get the same amount of satisfaction and enjoyment from making and eating them for less than half the effort—brilliant!

Instead of rhubarb use a similar quantity of apples, or apples and blackberries, or a combination of apples and canned fruit—cherries, mixed summer fruits, or apricots, for example—and add mixed spice, cinnamon, or ground cloves, according to taste. (But unlike some people whose secret is safe with me, I haven't got the cheek to make an apple crumble with canned apples and put cloves in it . . . )

As for the crumble mixture, add a couple of tablespoons of oatmeal or crunched-up cornflakes, or a smaller spoonful of ground almonds or desiccated coconut if you want to jazz it up a bit.

SERVES 4–6
2 pounds (1 kg) rhubarb
1 rounded teaspoon ground ginger
Sugar (Demerara, light brown, or white)
Golden syrup
8 heaping tablespoons all-purpose flour
1 stick (8 tablespoons) (113 g) butter

1. Preheat oven to 375°F (190°C). Trim the rhubarb stalks and wash and cut into 1 inch-long- (2 cm) pieces.
2. Put the rhubarb in a saucepan with the ginger, a couple of tablespoons of sugar, a very little cold water, and a modest dollop of golden syrup.
3. Simmer gently over a very low heat until the rhubarb is soft and the liquid syrupy, about 20 minutes, then transfer to a deep-sided ovenproof dish.

4. Make the crumble topping by sifting the flour into a large bowl, then adding the butter in small pieces and rubbing it in until the mixture resembles fine bread crumbs.
5. Stir another couple of tablespoons of sugar into the crumble mixture; loosely cover the fruit with the crumble mixture without pressing it down too hard and bake for about 20 minutes, until the topping is slightly golden.

### Poor Man's Apple Pie

1½ pounds (750 g) baking apples
Cornflakes
Brown sugar
Butter

SERVES 4–6

1. Preheat to 350°F (180°C). Peel, core, and thinly slice the apples and put a layer of fruit across the bottom of a medium ovenproof dish.
2. Add a layer of cornflakes, then sprinkle over 2 teaspoons of sugar and dot with a few small pieces of butter.
3. Add another layer of apples followed by the same amount of sugar and butter, building up the layers as described above until you run out of fruit.
4. Bake for about 20 minutes, until the apples are soft.

### Banana & Orange Trifle

This recipe is especially good if you like the idea of trifle but can't stand cold custard.

SERVES 4–6
1 package orange Jell-O
1 cup (250 ml) boiling water
1 small can mandarin segments, drained, juice reserved
1 jelly roll or angel food cake
2 small bananas
½ cup (125 ml) whipped cream for serving

1.  Put the Jell-O in a large measuring cup or a bowl with 1 cup (250 ml) of boiling water, stir until dissolved, then add the juice from the mandarin segments and 2 or 3 ice cubes to make the Jell-O up to just 1½ cups (375 ml). Allow to cool for about 10 minutes while you arrange the pieces of cake (or a package of ladyfingers) in a large glass bowl with the mandarin segments and chopped bananas.
2.  Pour 1 cup (250 ml) of the cool Jell-O over the cake and fruit and refrigerate.
3.  Leave the remaining ½ cup (125 ml) of Jell-O to cool completely—say another 5 minutes—then add ½ cup (125 ml) of whipped cream to the measuring cup.
4.  Carefully pour the cream-Jell-O over the trifle and return to the fridge to set for a couple of hours. Serve the trifle as it is or finish it off with whipped cream and decorate with fruit or grated chocolate.

## Bread & Butter Pudding

SERVES 4–6
10 slices of medium or thinly sliced white bread
Butter
½ cup golden raisins

1 cup (250 ml) milk
⅔ cup (150 ml) light cream
3 eggs
3 egg yolks
Vanilla extract, a few drops
3–4 heaping tablespoons superfine granulated sugar
Confectioners' sugar
Heavy cream for serving

1. Preheat oven to 350°F (180°C). Remove the crusts from the bread slices, lightly butter the bread on both sides, then cut the slices in half diagonally and arrange them in an ovenproof dish (preferably Pyrex).
2. Wash and dry the golden raisins and sprinkle over the bread.
3. Warm the milk and cream together in a small saucepan while you beat the eggs, egg yolks, vanilla, and superfine sugar in a bowl, then whisk in the warm milk and cream.
4. Pour the egg and milk mixture over the bread and raisins and gently press down with a fork or a potato masher, then leave the pudding to soak for up to half an hour (no less than 10 minutes).
5. Cover the dish with aluminium foil and place in a large roasting pan half-filled with hot water (make sure there's at least 1 inch [2 cm] between the level of water and the top of the dish). Bake the pudding for about 45 minutes.
6. Remove the foil and allow the pudding to cool for about 10 minutes before dusting with confectioners' sugar. Serve with thick heavy cream.

### Raspberry Ice Cream

This is no match for Ben & Jerry's, but it's still pretty good, especially compared with the cheapest supermarket store-brand stuff, and can be made (almost) as easily without an ice cream machine.

Make it around the same time as the Bread & Butter Pudding (page 143) and you'll be able to use up the leftover egg whites. (The really lazy way is to crush up four or five baked meringue nests and use instead of the egg whites.)

SERVES 4–6
½ pound (225 g) fresh raspberries
½ cup (125 ml) heavy cream
1 carton or can (14 ounces) (425 g) ready-made custard
8 ounces (250 g) plain yogurt
3 egg whites (or 4–5 meringue nests)

1. Briefly blend the raspberries to a rough puree or squash them up a bit with the back of a spoon.
2. Whip the heavy cream in a large mixing bowl with an electric hand mixer for a minute until it starts to thicken, but is still quite loose and sloppy, then stir in the custard and raspberries, mixing well to spread the fruit around and add color.
3. Add the yogurt and crushed meringue nests, or whisk the egg whites in a separate bowl, and fold them into the mixture.
4. Transfer the ice cream into the largest-size freezer bag (or a 2-quart container) and put it in the freezer for about 45 minutes.
5. After 45 minutes, take the ice cream out (stand the freezer bag in a bowl to give it some support) then stir the ice cream with a metal spoon, or whisk it for a few seconds with an electric hand mixer on the lowest setting before returning to the freezer.
6. After an hour, take the ice cream out again and repeat Step 5; breaking the ice cream up to prevent ice crystals forming.

7. Repeat this process three or four times—which is why it's better to start making the ice cream in the morning—then leave the ice cream in the freezer, taking it out to soften up a bit about half an hour before serving.

## Chocolate Mousse

Use granulated sugar if you haven't got confectioners' sugar, and if you want a cream instead of a lighter mousse, add a couple of tablespoons of heavy cream or crème fraîche after the egg whites.

SERVES 6

8 ounces (225 g) plain dark chocolate
1 teaspoon instant coffee, dissolved in 4 tablespoons boiling water
1 tablespoon sherry or brandy
4 eggs
1 level tablespoon confectioners' sugar
Whipped cream
1 tablespoon cocoa powder

1. Break the chocolate into pieces and melt in a bowl over a saucepan of boiling water with the dissolved coffee and sherry, stirring occasionally, while you separate the eggs.
2. Once the chocolate mixture is completely smooth, remove from the heat and let cool for a minute before you beat the egg yolks into the mixture.
3. Whip the egg whites with an electric hand mixer in a separate bowl until stiff. Add the confectioners' sugar, then beat for another minute until stiff enough to stand up in peaks.
4. Fold the beaten egg whites into the chocolate mixture and spoon into six glass bowls or ramekins.

5. Chill for at least 3 hours and serve with whipped cream and a dusting of confectioners' sugar and cocoa powder.

## Treacle Tart

Nowadays, treacle tarts tend to be made with golden syrup; originally they were made with black treacle, so this is a modern compromise between the two. Eaten cold on its own, treacle tart is delicious; warm with extra thick cream it's to die for.

SERVES 4–6
Shortcrust pastry
6 tablespoons golden syrup
2 tablespoons black treacle, or substitute molasses
1½ tablespoons (25 g) butter
1 lemon, juice and rind
1½ cups (125 g) homemade white bread crumbs
¼ cup (60 ml) milk

1. Preheat oven to 350°F (180°C). Make shortcrust pastry with 1¼ cups (150 g) all-purpose flour (*page 134*), then roll the pastry out to fit a lightly greased 8-inch (15 cm) loose-bottomed tart pan, saving the trimmings to re-roll and cut into 8 thin strips for the top of the tart.
2. Put the syrup, treacle, butter, and lemon juice and rind in a saucepan over a low heat for a few minutes to melt the butter and dissolve the syrup and treacle.
3. Fill the pastry shell to the top with the bread crumbs, then carefully pour over the warm liquid, starting from the outside edge and working slowly around to the middle of the tart so all the bread crumbs are covered.
4. Roll out the remaining pastry, cut into 8 thin strips, then

dunk them in a small bowl of milk, or brush them with the milk, and make a criss-cross pattern across the top of the tart, gently pressing the ends of each strip into the edge of the pastry crust. (Mix the milk with an egg yolk for a deeper glaze.)

5. Bake for 20–25 minutes until the filling is just set and the pastry is a light golden brown.

## Tiramisu

This shortcut version (what else?) of tiramisu can be made in one large bowl but looks prettier piled into individual glass dessert dishes; the quantities given here will make at least six, depending on the size of your glasses. Tiramisu also freezes well and keeps for at least two days in the fridge, meaning you can make it well in advance of a lunch or dinner party.

(Incidentally, this is one quick fix I don't feel the slightest bit guilty about since Gordon Ramsay and Jamie Oliver both have recipes for tiramisu made with ladyfingers [savoiardi biscuits] in their books!)

SERVES APPROXIMATELY 6
1 tablespoon instant coffee
4 tablespoons Tia Maria, brandy, or sherry
2 tablespoon superfine granulated sugar
1 cup (250 g) mascarpone
1 medium-sized carton (18 ounces) ready-made custard
1 package (200 g) of sugar-coated, dried ladyfingers (or Savoiardi biscuits)
4 ounces (100 g) plain dark chocolate, grated

1. Make 1 cup (250 ml) of coffee with the tablespoon of instant coffee; add the liqueur and sugar and stir.
2. Beat the cheese in a large mixing bowl with a wooden spoon until soft, then add the custard and blend thoroughly.
3. Dip the ladyfingers into the coffee, put them into the glasses (3 or 4 fingers per layer, per glass), then sprinkle a layer of grated chocolate and top with a couple of spoonfuls of the mascarpone mixture.
4. Repeat Step 3, saving a little of the grated chocolate to sprinkle on the top of each dessert at the end.

## English Fruit Fool

The cheat's way of making a fruit fool is not to fiddle around soaking and stewing fresh fruit—open a can or jar! Instead of prunes, use the same-size can of imported strawberries, pears, peaches, or frozen berries, and add a couple of tablespoons of sherry, a few drops of vanilla extract, or the finely grated rind of half an orange to the fruit, for variation.

SERVES 4–6

1 jar (about 410 g) ready-to-serve prunes in natural juice or syrup
1 small (425 g) carton ready-made custard
⅔ cup (150 ml) heavy cream

1. Tip the fruit into a bowl; slit the prunes down one side with a sharp knife and pick out the stones.
2. Puree the prunes in a blender or food processor with about half the juice or syrup from the jar, then return to the bowl and stir in the custard.

3. Whip the heavy cream in another bowl with an electric hand mixer until it's firm enough to hold its shape and stand up in stiff peaks, then fold into the prunes and custard, blending thoroughly.
4. Chill in the fridge for at least 2 hours.

## Spotted Dick

And here it is, hiding away at the end of the chapter for fear of being laughed at. It wouldn't be right to call this the *pièce de résistance* when Spotted Dick is English to the core—but will somebody please come up with another name for this sweet, simple, and genuinely delicious little pud, which is the perfect embodiment of everything a dessert should be, but, sadly, so reviled and sorely neglected. Delicious hot with lots of custard sauce, I also like it cold, straight from the fridge, when it's like a cross between a fruit bun and lardy cake.

There's no need to steam the pudding (this also applies to other suet puddings—jam roly poly, for instance) when baking takes a lot less time; just loosely cover the pudding with aluminium foil and put it in the oven. On the other hand, steaming gives the pudding a softer texture all through, whereas baking makes a crust around the outside. So if you want to steam it, wrap the pudding in a double layer of wax or parchment paper inside an old, clean tea towel and pull it into a crescent shape so it fits neatly into a large saucepan of boiling water, then steam it gently with the lid on for 1½–2 hours. (To get the pudding out, strain the water out of the saucepan with the lid half on, tip the pudding onto a flat surface and leave to cool for a few minutes before unwrapping.)

¾ cup plus 2 tablespoons (75 g) white bread crumbs
½ cup plus 2 tablespoons (75 g) self-rising flour

1 teaspoons baking powder
¼ cup (48 g) superfine granulated sugar
2 ounces (50 g) suet
6 oz (175 g) zante currants or golden raisins
½ lemon, finely grated rind and juice
¼ cup (60 ml) milk

1. Preheat the oven 375°F (190°C). Put a large piece of aluminium foil on a baking sheet, shiny side upwards.
2. Put the bread crumbs, flour, baking powder, sugar, suet, dried fruit, lemon rind, and juice in a large bowl, mix together, and make a well in the center.
3. Add the milk to the bowl and mix with a knife or tablespoon until the dough starts to come together, then finish pinching the dough together with the fingers of one hand.
4. Turn the dough out onto a floured surface and sprinkle with a little flour before kneading gently for a minute. Then shape the smooth dough into a fat roll approximately 6 inches (15 cm) long.
5. Place the spotted dick (there, I said it) on the baking sheet, cover loosely with another large piece of foil, shiny side inwards, and bake for about 45 minutes. Remove the top piece of foil 5 minutes before the end of cooking time if you want the pudding to have a harder, golden crust.

ALSO TRY ...
Strawberry Meringues.
Meringue nests filled with fresh strawberries in season (or canned fruit cocktail, peaches, or pears, any time) and topped with yogurt.
Orange Cups.
This was my mom's way of getting us to eat oranges when we were

very small. Just cut the oranges in half, segment the fruit with a sharp knife as you would with a grapefruit, then sprinkle with sugar and put a cherry in the middle.

Baked Banana Custard. Preheat oven to 300–325°F (150–160°C). Slice bananas in half lengthwise, pour over a pint of instant custard, sprinkle with brown sugar, and bake 20–30 minutes.

Fruit Jell-O. Make Jell-O with a can of fruit first thing in the morning (when you're already boiling water to make tea or coffee) and use the fruit juice to make the Jell-O up to 2 cups (500 ml). It should be set and ready to eat by dinnertime.

"I don't even butter my bread;
I consider that cooking."

—Katherine Cebrian

# 7
# Can't cook? Don't cook!

*However good your intentions, there are bound to be times when even putting toast under the grill seems too much like hard work when all you want to do is eat something and you just can't face another sandwich. Luckily, there are still a few options left . . .*

## Tips

Put little bowls of pumpkin and sunflower seeds or peanuts out to nibble in front of the television. Children especially enjoy the ritual of peeling and spitting out the shells and are much less likely to eat too many than they would be with salted nuts or chips.

Bread crumbs come in handy for so many things so never throw away the last few slices of a stale loaf; make them into bread crumbs by cutting the crusts off and whizzing a few slices at a time in the food processor or blender. (As a rough guide, one slice of bread makes about ¼ cup [25 g] of bread crumbs.) If you use very fresh bread leave the crumbs to dry out on a sheet of wax paper for about half an hour. Mix the remains of different types of bread and store in the freezer in old bread bags.

Buy frozen fruit from the supermarket (you'll find several variations); it's cheaper than fresh, defrosts very quickly, and is perfect for making ready-chilled fruit and vegetable smoothies.

Ready-made coleslaw can be slimy and revolting but packets of fresh grated coleslaw vegetables are pretty good if you haven't got time to make it from scratch; just add mayonnaise and yogurt with lemon juice and seasoning at home.

Whether you're very hungry or just peckish, you should be

able to find something here to tide you over to the next cooked meal.

Celery stalks cut in half and filled with peanut butter or cream cheese.

Slices of ham spread with soft cheese, rolled up, and eaten with chunks of tomato.

Rice cakes spread with peanut butter or cream cheese and slices of cucumber.

Flour or corn tortilla wraps filled with ham, grated cheese, and coleslaw—almost, but not quite a sandwich.

Quickest guacamole: avocados mashed with natural yogurt, seasoned, and served with carrot sticks and tortilla chips.

Smoked mackerel (with lots of lemon juice) and brown bread and butter.

Salad: lettuce, spinach, watercress, mustard and cress, cucumber, tomatoes, radishes, peppers, corn kernels, grated carrot, celery, avocado, cheese, ham, tuna, salmon, croutons . . .

Shrimp cocktails: Blend a couple of tablespoons of mayonnaise with the same amount of tomato ketchup and mix in the shrimp, then spoon them over shredded lettuce, spinach, or watercress, sliced cucumber, and chunks of avocado. Sprinkle with paprika and crushed up, ready-made croutons, if you have them.

Get those leftovers out of the freezer (soup, chili, spag bol, moussaka, shepherd's pie, lasagne, pasta sauce, fish pie, fish cakes, pancakes . . . ) and reheat in the microwave. That's not really cooking, is it? No.

### Smoothies

The possibilities are endless, so experiment—or buy a book. Here are a few tried and tested recipes to be getting on with.
· Mix 1 large or 2 small bananas, a generous handful of frozen

berries, and a glass of apple juice in a blender or food processor. Serves four.

· Take half a bag or bunch of curly kale, wash well, and put through a juicer with 2 lemons, cut into quarters. Very refreshing, however bad it sounds—and you just know it's doing you good.

· Half a ripe mango, 2 tablespoon plan yogurt, and a glass of fresh orange juice, blended.

· One large or 2 small bananas, 2 tablespoons plain yogurt, 1 scoop of vanilla ice cream, ½ teaspoon nutmeg, honey, to taste. Peel the bananas and put them in the blender with the rest of the ingredients (adjust the amounts according to taste) and blend for 2 minutes. Pour into tall glasses with plenty of ice.

· Two or 3 carrots, depending on size, a few stalks of celery, and a large glass of apple juice, blended on high for a minute.

### Isotonic Drink

If you're already addicted to sugary, fizzy, so-called sports drinks, this won't impress you much, but as a healthier and cheaper alternative, it's pretty good, and it does exactly the same job without damaging your teeth or your diet.

THIS FILLS A 500 ML BOTTLE OF WATER (ALMOST 2 CUPS)
2 cups (450 ml) water
¼ cup (50 ml) lemon or lime juice, or ⅛ cup (25 ml) of each
2 teaspoons sugar
1 small pinch of salt

"He who does not mind his belly,
will hardly mind anything else."

—Samuel Johnson

# 8
# Let them eat cake

*There can't be many things more disappointing than your average doughnut. Bland, tasteless dough, gritty sugar, a little squirt of jam, and it's all over. Even worse, if you get the little squirt of jam in the first mouthful there's nothing to look forward to. What else can you do except eat another one?*

Maybe the biggest myth about baking cakes, apart from the idea that it's only for sissies, is that it requires a considerable amount of time, patience, and skill when in fact the opposite is true; making your own cakes must be one of the easiest, most therapeutic, and rewarding pasttimes ever. Anyone can do it.

The cakes in this chapter are divided into three sections: things to make with your children just for the fun of it; wholesome cakes full of fruit, bran, oats, nuts, and seeds, which are healthy enough to eat for breakfast (although I'm not sure how to square that with the fact that I wouldn't normally eat the cakes in the first section for breakfast, even though some of them contain breakfast cereal); and special occasion cakes for when you have more time and feel like showing off a bit.

## READY, SET, BAKE . . .

*What You Need*

Everything here can be made just as easily in a blender or food processor, but I prefer my old hand-held electric mixer because it gives me a bit more control over the whole process and saves on cleanup. The only other things you need are a large mixing bowl, metal measuring spoons, a set of scales or measuring cups, and a couple of cake pans.

### Cake pans

A standard size 8×4-inch loaf pan is perfect for tea breads. For larger cakes I nearly always use two shallower 7-inch (18 cm) layer cake pans instead of one deeper pan; it's easier to judge the baking time that way and it dispenses with the hassle of cutting a much bigger cake in half if you want to fill it with jam or cream afterwards. Where a recipe requires one cake pan rather than a standard loaf pan or layer cake pans, an 8-inch (21 cm) round or square pan generally works well, although the one I use at home is actually a rectangular roasting pan with straight sides, roughly 8×10 inches (21 cm×28 cm) and about 1 ½ inches (3 cm) deep.

You can always use an old English biscuit pan instead of a cake pan, the only difference being that a biscuit pan won't be nonstick, so make sure you grease it well and line it completely with parchment paper. Biscuit pans make good substitutes when you want something more unusual—a heart-shaped or octagonal cake, for instance—and you can't find the pan you want in the shops.

### Lining the Pan

You don't have to fiddle around trying to make little bits of wax paper or parchment paper fit all four sides of the cake pan. A lot of cake recipes tell you to line the bottom of the pan, but I like to cut one long piece of paper that goes across the bottom of the pan and up two of the sides, leaving about an inch (2 or 3 cms) of surplus sticking up above the edge. This makes it easy to lift the cake straight out of the pan after baking; I've called it long-strip-lining in the recipes. For round cakes, draw a circle around the bottom of the pan straight onto the paper. If you're using two shallow layer cake pans you won't need to line the sides.

Grease cake pans with a different fat from the one you're using in the cake mixture; for example, if the recipe calls for butter, grease the pan with sunflower oil for a guaranteed nonstick result. Use crumpled wax paper (or paper towels if you're using oil) to grease the bottom and sides of the pan; then line the pan with the parchment or wax paper and lightly grease that, too.

### How to Tell When the Cake is Baked

Smaller, individual cakes should be soft and springy but firm to the touch. For larger cakes, insert a skewer or a very thin, sharp knife into the middle of the cake; if it comes out clean, the cake is ready. If the cake is baked on the outside but still a bit gooey on the inside (i.e., the skewer comes out streaked with raw cake batter), cover the top with a couple of layers of parchment paper or aluminium foil with the shiny side down to draw more heat towards the inside of the cake and let it bake a bit longer.

### Putting it in the Pan

Plastic spatulas are perfect for scraping the bowl—I keep meaning to get one—but any large spoon will do. For stickier cakes like Flapjacks, use a tablespoon and fork to get the mixture into the pan. Cakes naturally rise in the middle, so spread the mixture towards the sides of the pan and hollow it out slightly in the center.

### Getting it out of the Pan

After a minute or two of cooling, the cake will shrink away from the sides of the pan ever so slightly. Run a sharp knife around the edges and gently lift the cake out by holding the lining paper on either side. If you haven't got enough paper to get hold of, place a wire cooling rack over the top of the cake, carefully invert it, and ease the pan away from the cake.

### Measuring

You can buy a set of measuring spoons, scales, and measuring cups in any kitchen shop or large supermarket. Lots of the cakes in this chapter don't require the ingredients to be 100 percent accurate anyway, and even if they do, once you've learned what an ounce (or 25 g) of flour looks like you'll probably find you can do without a proper measuring tool altogether most of the time.

A heaping tablespoon = 1 ounces / 28 grams. Use the same size spoon every time you measure and you'll soon get the hang of it.

Finally, if you're not sure about size, fill a pan with flour and weigh that; e.g., a 1 pound loaf pan will hold 1 pound of flour.

### Approximate weights and measures

**SPOONS:**

1 teaspoon (1 tsp)................5ml

1 tablespoon (1 tbsp).........15 ml

**LIQUID MEASURES:**

¼ cup................................63 ml

½ cup (5 fl oz)...................125 ml

**DRY WEIGHTS:**

½ oz...................................15 g

1 oz...................................28 g

1⅜ oz................................40 g

1¾ oz................................50 g

2⅝ oz................................75 g

3½ oz (¼ lb) ..100–125 g

5¼ oz................................150 g

LIQUID MEASURES:

| | |
|---|---|
| ⅓ pint | 200 ml |
| 1 cup | 300 ml |
| 1½ cups | 400 ml |
| 2 cups (20 fl oz) | 500 ml |
| 4 cups | 1.1 liter |

DRY WEIGHTS:

| | |
|---|---|
| 6⅛ oz | 175 g |
| 8 oz (½ lb) | 225 g |
| ⅓ oz (¾ lb) | 350 g |
| 1 lb | 450 g |
| 1¼ lb | 550 g |
| 1½ lb | 675 g |
| 1¾ lb | 800 g |
| 2 lb | 900 g |

## For Best Results

Much as I love a shortcut, I always, always sift the flour; you get a much better result if it's sifted; it only takes a few seconds to push flour through a sieve and a few seconds more to rinse the sieve under the hot tap, so there's no point in skipping it.

Get to know your oven. (If you have a fan oven you may find you have to reduce the temperature in some recipes by about 10 degrees.) Always preheat your oven and bake cakes in the middle of the oven unless otherwise stated in the recipe.

## Tips

To "rub in" flour and fat, use only your fingertips and hold your hands high above the bowl to keep the mixture cool and light.

A niftier way of rubbing in (for some recipes) is to cream the butter and sugar with an electric hand mixer, just long enough to mix the two together (no need to spend time getting it pale and fluffy as you would for a sponge cake), then beat in the flour on the lowest speed for a few seconds until the mixture resembles fine bread crumbs.

If you think a sponge cake mixture is about to curdle, add 1 teaspoon of flour with each addition of egg.

For an even softer consistency, use confectioners' sugar instead of superfine granulated sugar in a sponge cake recipe.

Make baking powder by mixing 2 parts cream of tartar to 1 part baking soda.

Make a good substitute for self-rising flour by adding 1 teaspoon of baking powder to 2 cups (225 g) all-purpose flour.

Keep lemons at room temperature; before squeezing, press and roll them on a hard surface, which makes it easier to extract the juice. (As a rough guide, one large lemon makes approximately 2 tablespoons of juice.)

If you crack eggs straight into the bowl one bad egg can ruin the whole lot, so break them separately into a cup first and add them to the batter one at a time.

## COOKING WITH CHILDREN

I worked with primary school children for years when my own children were small and I never came across a single one, boy or girl, who didn't enjoy cooking as an activity. The downside of your children baking at school, especially with the very young ones, is you never know whose sticky little fingers have been where; anything can happen between the mixing bowl, the oven, and beyond, even if they've all been made to wash their hands first. (It's hard not to think about these things sometimes.) My elder son never failed to save me a nice big piece of whatever it was he made when he was little, so when his younger brother came along and kept his cakes all to himself without offering me so much as a bite—I breathed a huge sigh of relief.

At least when you're cooking at home you have a bit more control in the hygiene department, and anything you can do with

a class of twenty-five has to be easier in your own kitchen with only two or three children.

One of the great advantages of cooking with children of all ages, apart from getting them interested in food, is that doing something together in the kitchen creates a perfect, informal opportunity to talk, which can otherwise be quite hard to come by in the average household where everyone constantly rushes off in different directions all the time.

Not only that, if you get them interested early on, by the time your kids are teenagers they should be able to produce the occasional family meal themselves—although that probably won't include doing the washing up.

## Easy Cheesy Shortbreads

You'll find very cheap sets of cookie cutters shaped like animals, teddies, stars, and so on in supermarkets and kitchen shops. Buy at least two different sets; once you've got them, you'll be using them forever.

The thinner you roll out the dough, the crisper these shortbreads will be, so cut them out in varying thicknesses until you find out which way you like them best, or do some thick and some thin.

(Leave out the egg yolk if you like, it doesn't make a lot of difference—ditto the paprika.)

VARIABLE AMOUNT, DEPENDING ON SIZE OF CUTTER, AND
THICKNESS OF DOUGH . . .
¾ cup plus 1 tablespoon all-purpose (100 g) flour
1 teaspoon paprika
½ stick (4 tablespoons) (56 g) butter or margarine
¾ cup (50 g) grated cheese

Splash of milk

1 egg yolk, beaten

1. Preheat oven to 375°F (190°C). Sift the flour and paprika into a large mixing bowl; add the butter or margarine in little pieces and rub in with your fingertips until the mixture resembles rough bread crumbs.
2. Add the grated cheese, stir, then make a well in the center. Pour in the milk and egg yolk, and mix it all together to make a firm dough.
3. Put the dough on a floured surface and knead it for a bit, then divide the dough into two pieces. Wrap one half in plastic wrap and refrigerate while you roll out the other half.
4. Cut the shortbreads out, place on lightly greased baking sheets, and bake for 10–15 minutes, until they are a light golden brown.

### Cheese & Zucchini Scones

Any recipe for scones is very simple for children to make and these are much nicer than they sound, so don't be put off if you're not used to the idea of making cakes and cookies with grated vegetables; once upon a time we thought carrot cake was on the weird side; now it's as normal and accepted as a jam tart (page 167).

Traditionally, scones tend to be made with all-purpose flour, cream of tartar, and baking soda, but self-rising flour alone works brilliantly—and you don't need a rolling pin either—just pummel the dough out roughly with your hands, cut out the scones, then knead the remains together again, repeating the process until you run out of dough.

To make fruit scones, mix a couple of tablespoons of sugar and a handful of golden raisins (washed and plumped in warm

water) with the rubbed-in flour and butter before adding the milk.

MAKES ABOUT 12
2 cups (225 g) self-rising flour
Salt and pepper
¾ cup (50 g) grated cheddar cheese
1 zucchini, peeled
½ stick (4 tablespoons) (56g) butter or margarine
¼ cup (60 ml) milk

1. Preheat oven to 425°F (220°C). Sift the flour and seasoning into a large mixing bowl.
2. Grate the cheese and zucchini together on a dinner plate.
3. Add the butter in small pieces to the flour in the mixing bowl, rub in with your fingertips until the mixture resembles medium-fine bread crumbs, and make a well in the center.
4. Add the milk, grated cheese, and zucchini, and mix it all together to make a soft dough.
5. Turn the dough out onto a floured surface and knead for a minute, press out to about a 1-inch thickness, then cut into rounds with a pastry cutter, tumbler, or cup.
6. Place the scones on a greased baking sheet about 1 inch (2 cm) apart, glaze with milk, and bake for about 10 minutes, until the scones are risen and light golden brown on top.

## Jam Tarts

Yet another recipe where you only need approximate measurements, but if you want to weigh out the ingredients as part of the activity, just roughly translate the number of tablespoons into ounces or grams.

MAKES 12 (OR 18 MINIS) DEPENDING ON THE SIZE OF THE
PASTRY CUTTER
¼ cup (30g) all-purpose flour
2 tablespoons butter
1 tablespoon sugar
2 tablespoons milk
Milk for glazing
Jam, marmalade, or lemon curd

1.  Preheat oven to 375°F (190°C). Sift the flour into a mixing
    bowl and rub in the butter until the mixture resembles
    medium-fine bread crumbs.
2.  Stir in the sugar, then add the milk and mix together to make
    a firm dough.
3.  Turn the dough out onto a floured surface and roll it out to
    about 16-inch (1 mm) thick.
4.  Cut out rounds with a pastry cutter—or any cup that looks
    about the right size for the job—and place them in a greased
    muffin pan.
5.  Glaze each pastry circle with a little milk, then prick twice
    with a fork and put a teaspoon of jam in each one. (Don't
    overfill as the jam expands in the oven.)
6.  Bake for about 10 minutes, or until the pastry is a light, golden
    brown.

## Chocolate Rice Krispies Cakes

The favorite of old favorites; add mini marshmallows or brightly
colored sprinkles to make them more interesting—or raisins if
you're desperately trying to get your children to eat more fruit.
(Even if they usually pick the pieces of fruit out of everything,
it's always possible that they might eat some by mistake.)

MAKES APPROXIMATELY 24 CAKES
2 bars (4 ounces) (110g) each milk chocolate
Rice Krispies

1.  Melt the chocolate in a bowl over a saucepan of boiling water.
2.  Stir in the Rice Krispies; as many as possible, making sure they're all well covered in chocolate.
3.  Spoon the mixture into cupcake liners and leave to set for about an hour. (If it's very hot, keep them in the fridge.)

## Cornflake Cakes

½ stick (4 tablespoons) (56 g) butter or margarine
2 heaping tablespoons golden syrup
1 bar (4 ounces/110 g) milk or plain dark chocolate
3½ cups (100 g) cornflakes
⅓ cup (25 g) desiccated coconut

1.  Melt the butter, syrup, and chocolate in a bowl over a saucepan of boiling water.
2.  Add the cornflakes and coconut and mix well.
3.  Spoon into cupcake liners and leave to set for at least an hour. (As with Rice Krispies cakes, store them in the fridge if it's hot.)

## Cupcakes

There's no end to what you can use for decorating cupcakes, or fairy cakes as the English call them. Use M&Ms, chocolate buttons, jelly beans, hundreds and thousands, glacé cherries, walnuts . . . or just piping gel to make patterns on the icing.

Make butterfly cakes by cutting out a circle of cake from the center of each sponge cake, filling the holes with butter frosting, then cutting the circles in half and placing them on top of the butter frosting to look like wings. Finish by dusting with a little confectioners' sugar.

To make chocolate cupcakes, substitute 1 ounce (25 g) of cocoa powder for about 1 ounce (25 g) of the flour.

To make a Victoria sponge, grease and line two 7-inch (18 cm) layer cake pans and increase the quantities of the basic mixture by half, i.e., 6 ounces (150g) each of flour, butter, and sugar, and three eggs.

## MAKES ABOUT 24 CAKES

½ stick (4 tablespoons) (56 g) butter or margarine
½ cup (100 g) superfine granulated sugar
2 eggs, beaten
¾ cup plus 1 tablespoon (100 g) self-rising flour

1. Preheat oven to 375°F (190°C). Cream the butter and sugar in a large mixing bowl until pale and fluffy (this takes about 3 minutes with an electric hand mixer).
2. Gradually add the beaten egg to the mixture a little at a time and keep beating. If the batter starts to curdle (i.e., it looks lumpy and holey, a bit like cellulite—not your cellulite, someone else's), throw in a teaspoonful of the flour with each addition of egg.
3. Fold in the flour with a large spoon, making sure you've got it all in.
4. Spoon the mixture into paper-lined cupcake pans and bake for 10–15 minutes; the sponges should be a light golden color and firm and springy to the touch.

## FROSTING FAIRY CAKES

BUTTER FROSTING: *Roughly 1 part butter or margarine to 3 parts confectioners' sugar.*

1. Sift the confectioners' sugar into a large bowl with the butter, add 2 tablespoons of hot water, and beat it all together. Use a couple of drops of food coloring if you like, and if you think the frosting is still too thick, add a little more hot water a drop at a time until you get the consistency you want.

FOR THE GLACÉ ICING

Sift the confectioners' sugar into a large bowl and add a little lukewarm water very gradually, stirring all the time; roughly 1 tablespoon of water to 4 tablespoons of confectioners' sugar. Glacé icing can go from too heavy to pure liquid in seconds, so work slowly, but don't worry if you end up with runny icing; just sift in some more sugar until you've got it the way you want.

## Gingerbread Men

Again, measurements don't need to be exact—but don't be tempted to overdo the golden syrup, or the dough will become too soft and unworkable.

(Store in a airtight container with a tight-fitting lid to keep the gingerbread men from jumping out and running away.)

MAKES ABOUT 12 LARGE GINGERBREAD MEN

Zante currants
1½ cups (175 g) all-purpose flour
½ teaspoon baking soda
Pinch of salt
2 teaspoons ground ginger
2 tablespoons (30 g) butter or margarine
3 tablespoons (½ cup/85 g) light brown sugar
1 egg
1 tablespoon golden syrup

1. Grease two baking sheets and preheat the oven to 350–375°F (180–190°C).
2. Wash a big handful of currants in a sieve and leave them to drain on paper towels or an old, clean tea towel.
3. Sift the flour, baking soda, salt, and ginger into a large mixing bowl.
4. Rub in the butter with your fingertips until the mixture resembles medium-fine bread crumbs.
5. Mix in the sugar and make a well in the center.
6. Put the egg and golden syrup into the well, and use a fork to stir everything together to make a soft, pliable dough.
7. Turn the dough out onto a floured surface, knead for a minute until it feels ready, then roll out to about a ⅛-inch (3 mm) thickness.
8. Cut out as many gingerbread men as you can, and place them on the baking sheets, then roll out the remaining dough and cut out more. Keep going until you've run out of dough.
9. Press currants firmly onto the gingerbread men where you want their eyes, mouths, and buttons to be.
10. Bake the gingerbread men in the center and/or the top of the oven for 10–15 minutes, until they are crisp and golden.

## Sweetloaf

I wouldn't recommend using cooking chocolate for this. In fact I wouldn't recommend using cooking chocolate for anything, but any good-quality regular chocolate (i.e., Cadbury's, Green + Black, Ghiradelli brand) would be okay. Malted milk or rich tea biscuits are perfect, but digestives, Penguins, or Viscount Biscuits work equally well. Chopped hazelnuts and glacé cherries are also good, so use them instead of the marshmallows if you prefer—if you want nuts and cherries in addition to the marshmallows, reduce the amount of cookies.

For a grown-up version, make the sweetloaf with the best chocolate you can get your hands on and cut it into super-thin slithers at the end. It should look, and taste, good enough to give to guests with the coffee after dinner.

About 1½ pounds (675 g) milk chocolate
½ stick (4 tablespoons) (113 g) unsalted butter
A generous handful of raisins
8 rich tea or malted milk imported English biscuits, or other cookies
4 imported English ginger biscuits, or other ginger cookies
A generous handful of mini marshmallows

1. Very lightly grease and long-strip-line a standard (9 × 5-inch) loaf pan.
2. Break the chocolate into small pieces and put it in a bowl over a pan of boiling water to melt.
3. Melt the butter separately—in the microwave is good; about 40 seconds on the defrost setting—and never be tempted to try and melt the butter and chocolate together for this; for some reason it just turns into a thick, lumpy, unworkable mess.
4. Wash and dry the raisins; break up the biscuits or cookies on a dinner plate or in a bowl; add the dried fruit and marshmallows, and mix it all up together.
5. When the chocolate has melted, stir in the melted butter followed by the rest of the ingredients and pour the mixture into the lined loaf pan.

6. Leave to chill in the fridge for several hours, preferably overnight; cut into very thin slices and serve.

*Note: The colder and harder the sweetloaf becomes, the easier it is to cut into super-thin slices, which is why it's worth keeping it in the fridge for longer. Otherwise, cut thicker slices, then cut the slices into fingers.*

## Treacle Crunches

I love these; black treacle is a good source of iron and there's no added sugar, so I like to think these are a slightly healthier option than some of the other cakes in this section.

MAKES ABOUT 18 CRUNCHES

8 ounces (220 g) imported digestive biscuits (roughly 16 biscuits), or graham crackers

½ pound (about 225 g) milk chocolate

1 stick (8 tablespoons) (113g) butter or margarine

1 heaping tablespoon black treacle, or substitute molasses

1. Crumble the digestive biscuits into tiny pieces, using your hands, or bash them up with a heavy object; a mug or a rolling pin will do. Break the chocolate into squares.
2. Melt the butter in a bowl over a saucepan of boiling water, then add the black treacle.
3. Add the chocolate to the bowl and stir for a minute or two until it's thoroughly melted and there are no lumps left.
4. Mix the crumbled biscuits into the chocolate, then spoon the mixture into paper cupcake liners and leave to set in the fridge for about an hour.

## Chocolate Chip Cookies

You can buy chocolate chips in the baking section at the supermarket, but these are more fun if you use Smarties or M&Ms and crush them up yourself by putting them in a plastic ziplock bag, or something similar, and bashing them with a cup or rolling pin.

MAKES ABOUT 24 COOKIES

2 cups (225 g) self-rising flour

10 tablespoons (150 g) butter or margarine

½ cup (100 g) superfine granulated sugar

1 egg, beaten

2 ounces (50 g) broken M&Ms or chocolate chips

1. Preheat oven to 350°F (180°C). Sift the flour into a large mixing bowl, add the butter or margarine in small pieces, and rub in until the mixture resembles medium-fine bread crumbs.
2. Stir in the sugar, then make a well in the center. Add the beaten egg, and mix to a stiff dough.
3. Turn the dough out onto a floured surface and knead for a couple of minutes until smooth, then work in the M&Ms or chocolate chips. Wrap the dough in plastic wrap or aluminium foil and chill in the fridge for 30 minutes.
4. Roll out the chilled dough to about ⅛ inch thick (3 mm) and cut out the cookies with a pastry cutter or cup.
5. Place the cookies a little apart on greased baking sheets, prick them with a fork a few times, and bake for about 10 minutes, until golden.

# WHOLESOME CAKES

No matter how sugary, scrumptious, and inviting store-bought cakes appear to be on the outside they usually don't live up to your expectations, whereas what these wholesome cakes lack in the looks department, they more than make up for in taste, texture, and the sheer enjoyment of eating something sweet that's actually quite good for you.

## Carrot Cake

There are lots of methods for making carrot cake. I think this is probably the easiest and the result is a lovely moist cake that keeps in the fridge for a few days, assuming it's around that long. I use Quark, the virtually fat-free soft cheese for the topping, but you can use any other low-fat cream cheese, or even full-fat cream cheese if you prefer, it doesn't make much difference to the end result either way.

THE CAKE
1 orange, finely grated rind and juice
1 lemon, juice squeezed
2 sticks (16 tablespoons) (226 g) butter
1¼ cup (225 g) light brown sugar
4 eggs, whites and yolks separated
2 cups (225 g) self-rising flour
1 teaspoon baking powder
5 small or 3 large carrots, grated

THE FROSTING
3 tablespoons runny honey
8 ounces (225 g) cream cheese or Quark
Lemon/orange juice

OPTIONAL
⅓ cup (150 g) walnuts, broken into small pieces

1. Preheat the oven to 350°F (180°C). Grease the bottom of two 7-inch (18 cm) layer cake pans and line with wax or parchment paper.
2. Wash and cut the orange and lemon in half; put the finely grated rind of half the orange into a small bowl with the juice, plus the juice of one of the lemon halves. (Put the remaining halves of orange and lemon aside for the frosting.)
3. Cream the butter and sugar in a large mixing bowl, using a electric hand mixer, until pale and fluffy.
4. Beat in the eggs yolks and then add the lemon/orange juice and rind.
5. Fold in the flour and baking powder
6. Using a clean beater, whisk the egg whites until stiff and smooth looking (all the bubbles will disappear) and fold into the cake mixture, followed by the grated carrots and the walnut pieces if you're using them.
7. Divide the mixture equally between the prepared pans and bake in a moderate oven for about 45 minutes. Cool on a rack.
8. When the cakes are cool, remove from the pans. Beat the honey and cream cheese together with the remainder of the orange and lemon juice. Use half the frosting to sandwich the layers together and spread the rest on the top of the cake.

## Bran Loaf

More delicious than store-bought and so easy to fling together a child can do it. This must be one of the only cake mixtures that looks and tastes pretty revolting in the bowl, but honestly, the end result is well worth the complete lack of effort—best sliced thinly and eaten with butter or jam.

1 cup Kellogg's All Bran
1 cup (150 g) either zante currants, mixed dried fruit, or golden raisins
1 mug of milk
A generous ½ cup superfine granulated or light brown sugar
1 cup (120 g) self-raising flour

1. Preheat the oven to approximately 325°F (160°C). Put every-thing except the flour in a large bowl and leave the mixture to stand for about an hour.
2. Grease and long-strip-line *(see page 160)* a standard-size loaf pan.
3. Sift the flour into the soggy mixture; stir it in well, and pour the batter into the loaf pan, spreading it evenly up to the sides.
4. Bake in the preheated oven for about an hour and a half, un-til a skewer or sharp knife inserted into the middle of the cake comes out clean.

## Rock Cakes

These aren't much like the rock cakes I've found in the super-market, which were pale and flat with only about three raisins in each one. I use more fruit, slightly less fat, and *a lot* less sugar than I've found in other recipes, but these rock cakes are as good as any I've eaten—and I've got a sweet tooth. I like to use light brown sugar, but there's no reason why you can't use demerara, superfine granulated, or just plain granulated if that's all you've got.

MAKES ABOUT 24 ROCK CAKES
1 bag (1 pound/450 g) dried fruit
1 pound (450 g) self-rising flour
11 tablespoons (150 g) butter or margarine
⅓ cup (50 g) light brown sugar
1 teaspoon nutmeg
1 teaspoon cinnamon
1 teaspoon mixed spice
2 eggs, beaten
A big splash of milk

1. Preheat the oven to 400°F (200°C). Grease two baking sheets. Wash the fruit in warm water and assemble the rest of the ingredients.
2. Sift the flour into a very large mixing bowl and rub in the butter or margarine in small pieces.
3. Don't overwork the mixture; as soon as it vaguely resembles rough bread crumbs, add the sugar, spices, and fruit and mix it all together.
4. Make a well in the center and pour in the beaten eggs with a big of splash of milk, then gradually work the liquid into the mixture to make a stiff, moist, dough, adding another splash of milk if you think the dough is too dry.
5. Using a spoon and your fingers, shape the mixture into rocky lumps (roughly the size of ping-pong balls) on the greased baking sheets, and bake in the preheated oven for about 20 minutes until they're a light, golden brown.

## Ginger Cake

Ginger cakes are always best left for a couple days before eating, which gives them time to develop that lovely soft, sticky texture.

If you haven't got black treacle, use twice the amount of golden syrup; the end result will still be good, but a bit lighter in color and texture.

⅓ cup (113 g) golden syrup
*and*
⅓ cup (113 g) black treacle, or molasses or ⅔ cup (225 g) golden syrup
½ stick (4 tablespoons) (56 g) butter
¼ cup (55 g) lard
2 cups (225 g) all-purpose flour
¼ teaspoon baking soda
½ cup plus 1 tablespoon (100 g) soft dark brown sugar
1 teaspoon mixed spice
1 teaspoon ground ginger
A very little milk

1. Preheat the oven to 335°F (170°C) or slightly lower; this takes over an hour to cook and you don't want it to burn. Put the syrup and treacle in a small saucepan with the butter and lard on a very low heat while you assemble the rest of the ingredients and long-strip-line *(see page 160)* a square cake pan.
2. Sift the flour and baking soda into a large bowl with the sugar and spices, mix everything together and make a well in the center.
3. Pour the melted fat and syrup/treacle mixture into the center.
4. Beat the mixture well, starting in the center and working outwards to incorporate all the dry ingredients, adding just enough milk to make a thick, smooth batter.
5. Scoop the batter into the cake pan and bake near the bottom of the oven for 1–1½ hours until the cake is firm and dark brown.

6. Allow the cake to cool on a wire cooling rack, then wrap it up well in wax paper and aluminium foil, or store in an airtight container for a couple of days.

## Banana Cake

You can also make banana cake by following the recipe for a basic Victoria sponge (*see Fairy Cakes, page 169*); just use brown sugar instead of white and add the mashed bananas to the mixture after you've folded in the flour. There's not much difference between these two methods, except this one uses less butter and sugar, making the end result a bit lighter in texture and slightly less rich.

½ stick (4 tablespoons) (113 g) butter
2 cups (225 g) self-rising flour
½ cup plus 1 tablespoon (100 g) dark brown sugar
2 eggs
3–4 bananas, depending on size, mashed
Very little milk

1. Preheat the oven to 350°F (180°C). Grease and long-strip-line a square cake pan (or a loaf pan, although the top of the cake may split slightly in the standard loaf pan).
2. Gently rub in the butter and flour in a large bowl, using your fingertips and being careful not to overwork the mixture.
3. Stir in the sugar.
4. Add the eggs and the mashed bananas, beating well, and add a little milk to make a soft batter of dropping consistency.
5. Bake for about 45 minutes.

## All-In-One Apple Cake

I once met someone who told me she used to eat whole, raw cake mixtures before she could get them into the pan. I don't think I could, but if I was ever going to be tempted by an uncooked cake mixture, it would be this one.

5–6 sweet apples (not cooking apples)
½ cup plus 1 tablespoon (100 g) brown sugar
4 teaspoons cinnamon
1 teaspoon mixed spice
1¼ cups (150 g) self-rising flour
1 level teaspoon baking powder
½ cup (100 ml) sunflower oil
2 eggs

1. Preheat the oven to 375°F (190°C). Grease and line the cake or loaf pan with butter or margarine.
2. Cut the apples into quarters (or smaller) one at a time, peeling and removing the core and skin, then slice into small, fine chunks.
3. Mix the prepared apples with the sugar and spices, setting aside a few pieces to stick into the top of the cake, if you like.
4. Sift the flour and baking powder into a large bowl, make a well in the center; add the sunflower oil, eggs, and the spiced apples in no particular order, then beat the whole lot together on high speed with an electric hand mixer for half a minute.
5. Pour the mixture into the prepared pan and gently press the reserved pieces of apple into the top. Bake until a skewer inserted into the middle of the cake comes out clean, about 40 minutes.

## Bread Pudding

Make bread pudding in an 8-inch square (21 cm-square) cake pan or Pyrex baking dish; as long as you grease and long-strip-line it (*see page 160*) properly, either one will do.

8 slices bread from a large, white medium-sliced loaf
2 cups (500 ml) cold tea and 1 tea bag (if you're using a milder tea, use 2 tea bags)
8 ounces golden raisins
1 egg, beaten
½ cup plus 1 tablespoon (100 g) brown sugar
2 teaspoons mixed spice
Superfine sugar for sprinkling

1. Preheat oven to 375°F (190°C). Break the bread into tiny pieces with your hands (you don't need to remove the crusts if you're using soft, sliced bread) and put in a bowl with the cold tea. Mash the bread up well with a fork and leave it to stand for at least 10 minutes.
2. Mash again; add the fruit, beaten egg, brown sugar, and spice, and mix it all up. (The mixture should be nice and stodgy, but not too soggy.)
3. Put the mixture in the prepared pan, press down well, and bake for about 30 minutes, or until the cake is dark brown and firm to the touch. Set on a rack to cool. While it's cooling, sprinkle the top of the cake with a teaspoonful of superfine sugar.

## Flapjacks

Flapjack recipes, which are a type of English bar cookie, generally contain added sugar, but with so much sweetness in the mixture

I don't think you need it, especially if you include the dried fruit.

MAKES APPROXIMATELY 16 SMALL SQUARES
11 tablespoons (150 g) butter
6 tablespoons golden syrup
12 heaping tablespoons oatmeal

OPTIONAL
2 tablespoons dried fruit, chopped; apricots, dates, golden raisins

1. Preheat the oven to 325°F (160°C). Grease and long-strip-line a 7-inch (18 cm) square pan with parchment paper.
2. Melt the butter and syrup in a pan on the stove and put the oatmeal in a large mixing bowl.
3. Pour the melted butter and syrup over the oatmeal and mix together thoroughly (adding the dried fruit at this stage, if using). Make sure there are no dry lumps of oatmeal hiding in the middle of the mixture.
4. Press the mixture firmly into the lined pan, using the back of a fork to even it out, and bake for about 20 minutes.
5. Leave the flapjacks to cool for 10 minutes, then mark them into squares or slices with a sharp knife, then lift the whole lot out of the pan, using the lining paper.
6. After 40–45 minutes, cut the flapjacks up, then separate and leave to cool completely on a wire tray.

## Seed Cake

This is a very old recipe; the sort of thing your great-granny would have made between putting a week's-worth of washing through the wringer washer and making dinner for thirteen children. Perhaps this isn't quite as wholesome as some of the other cakes in this section, but caraway seeds are good for the digestion apparently, and if all else failed I'd sooner give a child a piece of homemade sponge than a cereal bar for breakfast.

Caraway seeds are slightly bitter, so although the vanilla extract isn't vital, putting it in will give the cake that little bit of added sweetness and flavor it needs.

12½ tablespoons (170 g) butter or margarine
1 scant cup (175 g) superfine granulated sugar
Vanilla extract, 1–2 teaspoons, according to taste
3 eggs, beaten
¾ cup plus 1 tablespoon (100 g) self-rising flour
¾ cup plus 1 tablespoon (100 g) all-purpose flour
2 teaspoons caraway seeds
Splash of milk

1. Preheat the oven to 340–350°F (170–180°C). Grease and *completely* line a 7- to 8-inch (18–21 cm) round cake pan.
2. Beat the butter, sugar, and vanilla together in a large mixing bowl until pale and fluffy.
3. Add the beaten eggs a little at a time, beating constantly to prevent curdling.
4. Fold in the flours and caraway seeds with a large metal spoon and add a splash of milk to get the mixture to a soft dropping consistency.
5. Scoop the mixture into the prepared pan and bake in the lower-middle half of the oven for 1 hour. Test the cake by inserting a skewer or sharp, thin-bladed knife in the center to see if it's ready; if the cake is baked on the outside but still a bit gooey

in the middle, put it back in the oven with a big piece of aluminium foil folded in fourths over the top to allow the cake to finish baking without burning.

## Plum Cake

This is a lovely cake with a soft texture and not too much sugar—even less if you use prunes in natural juice instead of syrup—so dust it with a couple of teaspoons of confectioners' sugar at the end if you like; it still counts as a wholesome cake in this book.

1 standard size jar ready-to-serve prunes in syrup or natural juice
1½ (175 g) self-rising flour
1 heaping teaspoon baking powder
1 teaspoon mixed spice
12 tablespoons (150 g) butter or margarine
½ cup plus 1 tablespoon (100 g) light brown sugar
2 eggs, beaten

1. Preheat the oven to 350°F (180°C). Grease and long-strip-line a 7-inch (18 cm) square cake pan.
2. Empty the jar of prunes into a bowl with the juice or syrup, split the prunes lengthwise and remove the stones.
3. Sift the flour, baking powder, and mixed spice together.
4. Cream the butter and sugar in a large bowl until pale and fluffy and gradually add the beaten egg with a teaspoon of flour each time to stop the mixture from curdling.
5. Add the prunes with the juice or syrup and blend on the slowest setting for just a few seconds to mix everything together without breaking up the fruit too much.
6. Fold in the flour with a large spoon, making sure it's com-

pletely incorporated, then scoop the batter into the prepared cake pan.

7. Bake in the middle of the oven for 30 minutes, or until a skewer or sharp knife, inserted in the center comes out clean, then lift the cake out of the pan and set aside to cool.

## Almond & Apricot Muffins

Unlike creamed sponge cakes, muffins don't need to be beaten to a super-smooth batter, so fold the butter and eggs in gently—just enough to get everything loosely combined—and try not to overwork the mixture.

Use whichever kind of dried fruit you want for these; the amounts don't have to be exact. There's no reason why you can't make muffins with fresh fruit either—blueberries and raspberries are ideal—but because I find blueberries too expensive unless they're on special, when I do buy them I always feel as if I ought to chew each one 32 times instead of squandering them in cake recipes.

If you do use fresh fruit and it's dripping in juice, gently strain off some of the liquid without pulping the fruit to mush, and reduce the amount of milk to prevent the mixture from ending up too soggy.

MAKES 16–24 DEPENDING ON SIZE
½ stick (4 tablespoons) (113 g) butter, melted
½ cup (125 ml) milk
1 large egg
2 cups (225 g) all-purpose flour
2 teaspoons baking powder
½ teaspoons baking soda
1 teaspoon salt

½ cup (100 g) superfine granulated sugar
4 ounces (100 g) dried apricots, finely chopped
⅔ cup (50 g) flaked almonds, broken up

1. Preheat the oven to 375°F (190°C). Melt the butter and set aside to cool.
2. Pour the milk into a measuring cup, add the egg, and whisk together with a fork.
3. Into a large mixing bowl, sift the flour, baking powder, baking soda, and salt. Add the sugar, chopped apricots, and broken almonds.
4. Make a well in the center, add the melted butter, the egg and milk mixture, and mix the whole lot together as sloppily as you like, for a lumpy, uneven batter.
5. Spoon the batter into a muffin pan lined with paper liners and bake for 10–12 minutes.

## Muesli Muffins

If you use completely unsweetened muesli you may want to add an extra tablespoon of light brown sugar.

MAKES 16–24 DEPENDING ON SIZE
½ stick (4 tablespoons) (113 g) butter, melted
½ cup (125 ml) milk
1 large egg
2 cups (225 g) plain whole wheat flour
2 teaspoons baking powder
½ teaspoon baking soda
1 teaspoon salt
1 teaspoon mixed spice
1 teaspoon cinnamon

½ cup plus 1 tablespoon (100 g) light brown sugar
1 cup muesli

1. Preheat oven to 375°F (190°C). Melt the butter and set aside to cool.
2. Pour the milk into a measuring cup, add the egg, and whisk together with a fork.
3. Into a large mixing bowl, sift the flour, baking powder, baking soda, salt, and spices (tipping the grains from the flour back into the bowl afterwards) and add the sugar and muesli.
4. Make a well in the center, add the melted butter, egg, and milk and mix the whole lot together as sloppily as you like, for a lumpy, uneven batter.
5. Spoon the batter into a muffin pan lined with paper liners and bake in the middle of the oven for 10–12 minutes.

## Pumpkin Muffins

This is the same method as the first two muffin recipes. It's hard to give an exact quantity for the pumpkin; so grate it before you start. Be careful when you're adding it to the mixture and leave some out if you think you've got too much.

MAKES 16–24 DEPENDING ON SIZE
½ stick (4 tablespoons) (113 g) butter, melted
½ (125 ml) milk
1 large egg
2 cups (225 g) all-purpose flour
2 teaspoons baking powder
1 teaspoon salt
½ teaspoon baking soda
½ cup (100 g) superfine granulated sugar

½ small pumpkin, grated
1–2 tablespoons crushed pumpkin seeds

1. Preheat oven to 375°F (190°C). Melt the butter and leave to one side to cool.
2. Pour the milk into a measuring cup, add the egg, and whisk together with a fork.
3. Into a large mixing bowl, sift the flour, baking powder, salt, and baking soda, then add the sugar and give it a good stir.
4. Make a well in the center, add the melted butter, egg, and milk and mix the whole lot together just a little before carefully adding the grated pumpkin and loosely combining to a lumpy, uneven mixture.
5. Add the crushed pumpkin seeds to the mixture, or add some and save the rest for the top of the muffins.
6. Spoon the mixture into a muffin pan lined with paper liners. Sprinkle with the crushed pumpkin seeds, and bake for 10–12 minutes.

# SPECIAL CAKES

Maximum effect for minimum effort; that's what you want when you're making a cake for a special occasion. Even though the end result should look pretty spectacular, all the cakes in this section are easily achievable, or they wouldn't be in this book. Trust me.

## Jelly Roll

Jelly roll, sometimes called a Swiss roll, is very straightforward to make, contains only a very few cheap ingredients, and can easily be turned into something special; a Chocolate Yule Log for Christmas (page 194) or a Caterpillar Cake (page 193), for instance. There's no butter in the mixture either so if you fill your Swiss roll with jam and/or a low fat-free cream cheese instead of whipped cream, it's pretty low in calories, too.

Make jelly rolls in a standard-size jelly roll pan (the one I use is 15×11×1-inch) and line the pan *completely* so the parchment paper comes about an inch (2 cm) above all four sides of the pan, then snip out the corners so there aren't any little folds of paper left to get stuck into the cake mixture, making the paper impossible to get off without tearing the sponge, once it's baked.

3 eggs
½ cup (100 g) superfine granulated sugar
¾ cup plus 1 tablespoon (100 g) all-purpose flour
2 tablespoons hot water

1. Preheat the oven to 400°F (200°C). Grease and line a jelly roll pan *(see page 160)*.
2. Using an electric mixer, whisk the eggs and sugar in a bowl until the mixture is thick, pale, and creamy and more or less double in size. This takes between 5 and 10 minutes, depending on the type of mixer you're using. (Don't even attempt to do this by hand unless you're supernaturally strong with the patience of a saint.)
3. Gently fold half the flour into the mixture (or flour plus cocoa if you're making a chocolate roll), followed by the hot water, then the rest of the flour, taking care not to beat the mixture; it should be a soft, smooth dropping consistency.
4. Scrape the batter into the prepared pan, tilting the pan to help spread the batter out evenly.
5. Bake for about 10 minutes until the sponge is risen, slightly golden, and springy to the touch. This cake cooks quickly, so

don't go off and do something else; get ready for the next stage.

## ROLLING IT UP

1. Wet a tea towel (an old, thin, threadbare one works best) then tightly wring it out so it's only slightly damp and lay it on a clean surface. Lay a clean sheet of wax paper (at least a couple of inches larger than the cake) on top of the damp tea towel and sprinkle it with sugar.
2. Turn the baked sponge out onto the clean, sugared wax paper and carefully peel off the old lining paper from the bottom of the cake.
3. Working as quickly as you can and without tying yourself up in knots, trim the crusty edges off the cake with a sharp knife. Now flip the wax paper over the short end of the sponge nearest to you and, starting with a tight fold, gently but firmly roll the whole thing up with the wax paper and damp cloth inside. Set aside to cool for about half an hour.

## TO FILL WITH JAM OR LEMON CURD

You can do this while the cake is still warm, so have the jam or lemon curd ready when the cake comes out of the oven; spread it over the warm cake as soon as you've peeled the lining paper off, then roll the cake up in the usual way.

## TO FILL WITH CREAM

If you're filling the roll with butter cream frosting, fresh whipped cream, or a combination of jam and cream, roll the cake up in the way described above; then when it's cool, carefully unroll the cake—you don't need to flatten it out completely—spread the filling over the cake and roll it back up without the wax paper and tea towel.

ALSO TRY . . .

Chocolate Jelly Roll.

To make the chocolate roll, instead of ¾ cup plus 2 tablespoons (100 g) flour, use ½ cup plus 2 tablespoons (75 g) flour and 1 ounce (25 g) of cocoa powder.

## Caterpillar Cake

There's more than one way of frosting a caterpillar cake, so use the suggestions below as a rough guide—you'll probably come up with better ideas of your own. Unless you're one of those mums so brilliant at cake decorating she could give up the day job and turn professional, it's a good idea to make your kids a novelty cake when they're still young and uncritical enough to appreciate your efforts. If your finished caterpillar isn't as good looking as you hoped it would be, pretend it's a worm that's just crawled out of the earth, put it on a plate, and surround it with Rice Krispies cakes (page 168).

INGREDIENTS GREEN CATERPILLAR

Jelly roll (page 190)

Glacé icing (page 171)

Green food coloring

Licorice Allsorts, or other licorice candies including
thin strands

Chocolate buttons

Chocolate marshmallow teacakes

1. Make glacé icing in the usual way (*see Notes, page 171*) and add 1 or 2 drops of coloring to get the shade you want. Keep the icing on the thin side so you can pour and spread it over the cake roll easily; if it's a bit too thin and you can see the cake

through it, wait for the icing to dry, then make more icing and repeat the process. I transfer the caterpillar to the cake board or plate now, rather than risk an accident at the end when the damage will be harder to disguise.

2. Before the icing has dried completely, stick the chocolate buttons along the caterpillar's back to make little spikes (or lay them flat, like spots), cut the marshmallows in half and place them at regular intervals along the bottom of the cake, 4 on each side, like little feet, and use 2 licorice strands to make the antennae. Pink and yellow Allsorts with a round bit of black licorice in the middle make good eyes and mouths; use different colors for each and slice them in half if you think they're too thick.

ALSO TRY...

For a chocolate caterpillar, make a chocolate butter frosting or melt cooking chocolate and add a couple of spoonfuls of cream when the chocolate starts cooling. Make the easy chocolate frosting (*page 198*) or use a ready-made chocolate frosting from the baking section at the supermarket, although you might find it's a bit harder to spread all over the cake without making a mess of the sponge.

Use M&Ms, gum drops, or mini marshmallows to decorate the caterpillar's back instead of chocolate buttons.

Color the glacé icing with pink, yellow, or orange food coloring.

## Chocolate Yule Log

Rather than have a too-small log, I make two cake rolls and use one to make a branch and add a bit of length to the other, in which case you'd need to double the quantities below.

3 eggs
½ cup (100 g) superfine granulated sugar
½ cup plus 2 tablespoons (75 g) all-purpose flour
⅓ cup (25 g) cocoa powder

1. Make 1 or 2 chocolate Jelly Roll (page 190).
2. If making only one cake roll, leave the cake roll as it is, or cut a piece diagonally about 1½ inches (4 cm) from one end, which you can attach to the side of the log with frosting to make it look like a branch.
3. Make plenty of chocolate butter frosting *(see Notes, page 170)* to fill and cover the log completely, marking the frosting with a fork, to resemble bark.
4. Stick a robin or a snowman, or something festive, on top of the cake, and finish at the time of serving with a dusting of sifted confectioners' sugar to look like snow.

## Layer Cake

2 cups (225 g) all-purpose flour
1 teaspoon baking powder
2 sticks (16 tablespoons) (226 g) butter or margarine
4 eggs
4 tablespoons hot water

1. Make the jelly roll in the usual way *(see page 190)*; turn it out of the pan and leave to cool on a wire cooling tray, covered with a damp cloth.
2. Cut the roll *horizontally* into four strips of the same size and spread the each strip with whatever filling, or combination of fillings, you want to use.

3. Roll the first strip up; roll the second strip around the first one, followed by the remaining strips, pressing gently but firmly to seal the edges as you go.
4. Cover the cake with a thick frosting *(see page 170)* to disguise the seams and edges.

## Honey, Lemon & Yogurt Cake

Like banana cake, carrot cake, gingerbread, and fruit muffins, this is the type of thing you find in trendy cafés, where one slice of cake costs more than the whole thing would to make at home. It's really just a basic creamed sponge mixture with ideas above its station, but because it's so fragrant and delicious and has such a lovely soft texture, I think it deserves its place with the other special cakes.

### THE CAKE
12½ tablespoons (175 g) butter or margarine
¾ cup plus 2 tablespoons (175 g) superfine granulated sugar
1 lemon, juice and zest
3 eggs, beaten
1½ cups (175 g) all-purpose flour
1½ teaspoons baking powder
4 level tablespoons plain yogurt
2 teaspoons honey

### THE TOPPING
1 lemon, juice and zest
¼ cup (50 g) superfine granulated sugar
1–2 tablespoons confectioners' sugar

1. Preheat the oven to 350°F (180°C). Grease and *completely* line an 8-inch (21 cm) round cake pan.

2. Cream the butter, sugar, lemon juice, and zest in a large mixing bowl until pale and fluffy.

3. Gradually add the beaten eggs a little at a time, taking care not to curdle the mixture.

4. Sift the flour and baking powder into the bowl, followed by the yogurt and honey, and fold it all in together with a metal spoon as quickly as you can without overbeating the mixture.

5. Scoop the mixture into the prepared pan and bake *on one of the lower shelves of the oven* for about 1 hour.

6. Make the topping when the cake is still warm by mixing the juice and zest of the second lemon in a small saucepan with the sugar and heating for a few minutes until the sugar dissolves and becomes a clear syrup. Sprinkle the syrup evenly over the top of the cake. Just before serving dust the cake with sifted confectioners' sugar. Equally delicious warm or cold.

## The Ultimate Chocolate Cake

Don't use cooking chocolate or any of the bars of chocolate-flavored coating you find in the supermarket's baking section. Regular eating chocolate with between 40–60 percent cocoa solids (look at the list of ingredients on the wrapper) is much better for this cake. It doesn't have to be expensive either; most of the big supermarkets carry reasonably good plain chocolate at around $2 for a 4-ounce (100 g) bar. For an extra-moist sponge, add a couple of tablespoons of plain yogurt at the same time as the eggs, sugar, and melted chocolate—but don't overdo it or you'll end up with a pudding instead of a cake.

2 sticks (16 tablespoons) (226 g) butter or margarine

8 ounces (225 g) plain dark chocolate

2 heaping teaspoons instant coffee, dissolved in 2 tablespoons boiling water

2 tablespoons golden syrup

1½ cups (175 g) self-rising flour

1 teaspoon baking powder

⅔ cup (50 g) cocoa powder

1¼ cups (225 g) light brown sugar

3 eggs, beaten

### THE CHOCOLATE FROSTING

4 ounces (100 g) plain dark chocolate

2 tablespoons (28 g) butter

1 tablespoon golden syrup

1⅞ cups (225 g) confectioners' sugar

¾ cup cocoa powder

1 egg

### FOR THE CAKE

1. Line the bottom of two 7-inch (18 cm) layer cake pans. Preheat the oven to 350°F (180°C).
2. Melt the butter and chocolate (both broken into small pieces) with the dissolved coffee and golden syrup in a heatproof bowl over a pan of boiling water.
3. Meanwhile, sift the flour, baking powder, and cocoa powder into a large mixing bowl and make a well in the center.
4. Add the sugar, beaten eggs, and the thick melted chocolate mixture to the well and whisk everything together on maximum speed of an electric mixer for about 30 seconds to make a batter with a smooth, fudgy texture.

5. Divide the batter equally between the two prepared pans and bake in the middle (or lower and middle shelves if you can't fit both pans on the same shelf) of the oven for 20–30 minutes, until the sponges are risen and firm to the touch.

6. Allow to cool slightly while you make the chocolate frosting, then fill and cover the cake and store in an airtight container. This cake keeps well for at least a week.

FOR THE CHOCOLATE FROSTING

1. Melt the chocolate, butter, and syrup in a bowl over a pan of boiling water.

2. Sift the confectioners' sugar and cocoa powder together into a large mixing bowl and make a well in the center.

3. Pour the melted chocolate mixture into the well with the egg (or, if the bowl is big enough, add the dry ingredients and the egg to the chocolate mixture) and beat on high speed with an electric mixer for about 30 seconds until you've got a thick, smooth icing.

4. Fill and cover the cake, using a flat knife or a fork to make swirls in the frosting on the top and sides of the cake.

### Chocolate Caramel Cakes

THE SHORTBREAD

12½ tablespoons (175 g) butter
½ cup (100 g) superfine granulated sugar
2⅔ cups (300 g) all-purpose flour

THE FILLING

½ stick (4 tablespoons) (113 g) butter
2 cans (450 g each) condensed milk (about 2 cups)
4 tablespoons golden syrup

THE TOPPING
12 ounces (300 g) plain dark chocolate
⅔ cup (150 ml) light cream

FOR THE SHORTBREAD
1. Preheat the oven to 350°F (180°C). Grease a baking sheet.
2. Cream the butter and sugar together in a large mixing bowl for no more than a minute. (You're not making a sponge cake so it doesn't have to be especially pale and fluffy.)
3. Add the flour and beat on the lowest speed setting, using an electric mixer, for another minute until the mixture resembles medium-fine bread crumbs.
4. Press the shortbread dough into the baking sheet and bake for 10–15 minutes. Don't let the shortbread brown; it should still be only just golden.

FOR THE FILLING
1. Put the butter in a large saucepan over a low heat; when it's melted add the condensed milk and the golden syrup and heat gently for a couple of minutes until the ingredients are blended, stirring all the time.
2. Turn the heat up and bring to a boil (not too fiercely or you'll get splashed with very hot syrup—and it is dangerous) for 5–10 minutes, stirring or whisking with a small hand whisk all the time, until you have a light golden brown caramel.
3. Remove from the heat and let the caramel cool slightly for a minute or two, then pour and spread over the shortbread base and leave to cool completely for at 30 minutes.

FOR THE TOPPING
1. Melt the chocolate in a bowl over a pan of boiling water and stir in the cream.

2. Pour and spread over the cool caramel and shortbread base with the back of a spoon, making swirling patterns in the chocolate. When the chocolate is starting to set, mark into squares, and when the shortbread is cool, cut completely, lifting the chocolate caramel shortbread cakes off the pan with a flat knife. Store the shortbreads in an airtight container.

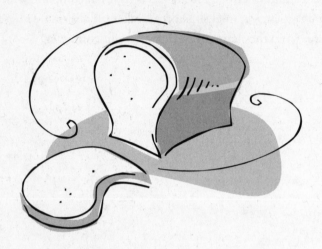

"When you cook, it should be an act of love. To put a frozen bag in the microwave for your child is an act of hate."

—Raymond Blanc

# 9
# Not only but also

*There's nothing here that you can't buy in the shops . . . so why bother? Well, all I can say is, if you can make something better yourself and save money at the same time, it's got to be worth having a go.*

Do your bit to help foil the food manufacturers' evil plan to put a morbidly obese child in every classroom. Leave those oven-ready hash browns in the supermarket, reject that dodgy potato salad, don't eat hot cross buns before Easter, and do try these at home.

## Quick Brown Bread

This is perfect for those of us who like the idea of baking our own bread but know we'll never get round to doing it properly. Don't be too heavy handed with the syrup—I've said this in some of the other recipes with golden syrup because, for me, the temptation to ladle it out of the pan in great dollops or squeeze the bottle too hard is overwhelming—otherwise the bread will be too soft and break up easily when you try and cut it. (Turn the loaf upside down when you slice it, in any case. It works better this way for some reason.)

2 cups (225 g) whole wheat flour
2 cups (225 g) all-purpose flour
1 teaspoon salt
1 teaspoon baking soda
1 teaspoon cream of tartar
½ cup (125 ml) milk

½ cup (125 ml) boiling water
1 tablespoon golden syrup
1 teaspoon vinegar

OPTIONAL
Crushed sunflower, pumpkins, or sesame seeds for sprinkling

1. Preheat the oven to 375°F (190°C). Liberally grease a standard 9×5-inch loaf pan.
2. Sift all the dry ingredients into a very large mixing bowl, tipping the grains from the whole wheat flour back into the bowl afterwards, and mix them together and make a well in the center.
3. Pour the milk into a measuring cup and fill with boiling water straight from the kettle to the ¾ pint (375 ml) mark.
4. Add the golden syrup and vinegar to the hot liquid and stir for a few seconds to dissolve the syrup.
5. Pour the liquid into the well and mix all the ingredients together with a large spoon to make a loose, sticky dough.
6. Scoop the dough into the prepared loaf pan and use the back of the spoon to push it down and spread it out as evenly as you possibly can. Sprinkle the seeds on top, if you're using them, and bake in the middle of the preheated oven, for 30–40 minutes.
7. Turn the loaf out of the pan and tap the bottom; a hollow sound means it's done.

## Soda Bread

This isn't the best bread for toast and sandwiches, but on its own with butter, or as something to have with soups and stews, it's great. (It also keeps for a couple of days wrapped in aluminium foil and freezes well.)

If you want to add any of the herbs or seeds listed below, mix them in with the dry ingredients at the beginning and reserve a bit to scatter across the top just before the loaf goes into the oven.

2⅔ cups (300 g) self-rising whole wheat flour
¾ cup plus 1 tablespoon (100 g) self-rising white flour
2 tablespoons (25 g) brown sugar
1 teaspoon salt
2 teaspoons baking soda
2 tablespoons (25 g) butter
½ cup (125 ml) milk
8 ounces (260 g) plain yogurt
½ cup (50 g) oatmeal

OPTIONAL
2 teaspoons dried (or 2 sprigs of fresh) rosemary, thyme, or sage
2 teaspoons seeds (pumpkin, sunflower, caraway) roughly chopped

1. Preheat the oven to 350°F (180°C). Grease a standard baking sheet.
2. Mix the dry ingredients together in a large bowl; add the butter in small pieces and rub in, then make a well in the center.
3. Mix the milk and yogurt together and pour most of the liquid into the well, reserving a couple of tablespoonfuls back for brushing over the top of the finished loaf.
4. Mix the liquid in quickly using your hands to make a soft (but not too sticky) dough, then turn the dough out onto a floured surface. Knead it very lightly for a minute and form into a round cottage-style loaf.

5. Place the loaf on the greased baking sheet and cut a deep cross into the top. Brush the remaining the milk/yogurt mixture all over the surface (you can use your hands if you don't have a pastry brush) and sprinkle over the oatmeal, or whatever other herbs or seeds you want to use, if any.
6. Bake in the oven for 30–40 minutes and allow the loaf to cool for half an hour before slicing and eating.

Note: *If you cannot locate self-rising whole wheat flour add 1–1½ teaspoon baking powder and a pinch of salt to regular whole wheat flour.*

## Garlic Bread

Garlic bread works best with baguettes but there's nothing to stop you from warming up any other type of bread at the bottom of the oven, wrapped in aluminium foil, then spreading it with garlic butter, once the bread's hot enough to melt the butter.

1 stick (8 tablespoons) (113 g) butter
2 garlic cloves
¼ teaspoon salt
1 baguette

OPTIONAL
2 teaspoon chopped parsley
Black pepper

1. Preheat oven to 400°F (200°C). Take the butter out of the fridge for a few minutes first to soften it up; crush the garlic and beat with the butter.
2. Make one long cut along the length of the baguette under-

neath and spread the loaf liberally with the garlic butter on both sides. Sprinkle with parsley and black pepper, if you like.

3. Turn the loaf up the right way and make deep, regular cuts all the way across the top, about halfway down to the bottom.

4. Wrap the loaf in aluminium foil and warm in the bottom of a hot oven, preheated to 400°F (200°C) for about 15–20 minutes, removing the foil 5 minutes before the end of the baking time for a crunchier crust.

## Guacamole

2 large avocados
1 or 2 tablespoons canned chopped tomatoes
½ teaspoon chili powder or cayenne pepper
1 clove garlic, crushed
1 tablespoon plain yogurt
Lime juice to taste (about 2 teaspoons)

Mash the avocados in a bowl, add the rest of the ingredients, and mix well. Cover with a layer of plastic wrap. The guacamole will keep refrigerated for up to 2 days.

## Hummus

⅔ cup (100 g) sesame seeds
1 can chickpeas (about 14.5 ounces /410 g)
2 tablespoons olive oil
2 cloves garlic
3 heaping tablespoon yogurt
Juice of 2 lemons, or 4–6 tablespoons lemon juice, according to taste
Salt and pepper

1. Put the sesame seeds and olive oil in a blender or food processor and whiz for about a minute, scraping down the sides once or twice if you need to.
2. Drain the can of chickpeas and add them to the blender with the rest of the ingredients, in no particular order, and blend on high speed for a couple of minutes.
3. Taste and adjust the seasoning and chill in the fridge for a couple of hours before eating. Keeps for about 1 week.

### Roasted Nuts

A great alternative to heavily salted and (smelly) dry-roasted peanuts.

Large bags of unsalted nuts can be found in local Asian shops and the international section of most major supermarkets. If they haven't already been shelled and peeled you can blanch them at home by soaking them in a bowl of boiling water for a few minutes, then straining through a colander, and plunging them into cold water, so the skins slide off easily.

For 1 pound (500 g) of nuts—cashews, peanuts, almonds or hazelnuts—use 2½ tablespoons (37 g) of butter, 1 teaspoon of salt, and any one of the following three seasonings:

1 tablespoon curry powder
1 tablespoon paprika
1 teaspoon chili powder
2 teaspoons ground cumin

1. Preheat the oven to 300°F (150°C).
2. Melt the butter on a roasting pan or large ovenproof dish, mix well with the spices, then add the nuts and give the pan a good shake, to coat all the nuts in the seasoned butter.

3.  Roast the nuts in the preheated oven for about 30 minutes. Allow to cool and store in an airtight container.

## Mayonnaise

Making mayonnaise is such a cinch, it's worth doing at home at least some of the time (especially in the summer when you're eating lots of salads) so when some beady-eyed domestic goddess asks if you made it yourself you can truthfully say yes.

Although you're supposed to use dry mustard I always buy prepared and use it straight from the jar, and it's fine.

3 egg yolks
½ teaspoon prepared English mustard
Salt and white pepper
3–4 tablespoons cider vinegar
2 tablespoons lemon juice
1 cup (250 ml) olive oil

1.  Put the yolks in a cold bowl with the mustard, salt, and white pepper; mix the vinegar and lemon juice together in a cup.
2.  Beat the egg yolks, using an electric hand mixer, for a minute, then start adding the oil, drop by drop to prevent the eggs curdling. Once the mayonnaise starts to thicken the oil can be added in a steady stream—but don't stop beating.
3.  Add half the vinegar and lemon juice as soon as the mayonnaise starts getting too thick to work with; then carry on adding the rest of the oil.
4.  Beat in the remaining vinegar and lemon juice—the mayonnaise should be thick and smooth. Taste and adjust the seasoning, adding more vinegar if you like a runnier texture

(although this makes it like a British salad cream rather than mayonnaise).

## Potato Salad

Use about half the quantity of mayonnaise made from the above recipe for this amount of potatoes, mixed with a couple of table-spoons of plain yogurt.

SERVES 6–12
2 pounds (1 kg) potatoes
Mayonnaise
Plain yogurt
Lemon juice
3 scallions, chopped
Fresh chives
Fresh parsley
Salt and pepper

1. Wash and boil the potatoes in their skins until just soft, then leave to cool for a few minutes. (Either remove the skins while the potatoes are still warm, or leave them on.)
2. Dice the potatoes and add to a large bowl with the mayonnaise, yogurt, lemon juice, chopped scallions, herbs, salt, and pepper. Mix gently and adjust the seasoning and consistency according to taste.

## Hash Browns

Hash browns are high in fat wherever they come from, although homemade ones less so, and they also contain more of the healthier ingredients per portion.

It goes without saying that they taste better too. (Add chopped fresh chives or parsley to the raw mixture to prove you didn't get them out of a package.)

THIS IS ENOUGH FOR ABOUT 16 GOOD-SIZE HASH BROWNS
2 pounds (1 kg) potatoes
1 onion
3 tablespoons all-purpose or whole wheat flour
3 tablespoons butter, melted

1. Peel and grate the potatoes, then wash well in a colander to rinse the starch away and squeeze dry in an old, clean tea towel.
2. Grate the onion and mix with the grated potatoes in a large bowl.
3. Sift the flour into the bowl, add the melted butter, and mix all the ingredients together.
4. Pat the mixture into cakes with your hands and shallow-fry in very hot oil for a few minutes on each side, flattening them out a bit with a spatula.

TO FREEZE
1. If you want to freeze hash browns, cook them first, drain on paper towels, and allow to cool. Then layer with wax paper, place in a large ziplock bag, and freeze.
2. Reheat straight from the freezer by placing the hash browns on an baking sheet and baking in the oven preheated to 425°F (220°C) for 15–20 minutes.

## Hot Cross Buns

Hot cross buns are nowhere as special as they used to be when you could only buy them on Good Friday, but as they're easy enough to make at home I think it's worth making them once, or even twice a year. There's no time to put your feet up; you need to move straight from one stage to the next, but having said that, the whole process is very straightforward and only takes about an hour from start to finish.

I made hot cross buns for the first time last Easter after my son made them at school and gave me a rough idea of the recipe at home. Although they weren't much like the store-bought variety they were still good but I don't know how his buns turned out because he didn't save one for me!

MAKES ABOUT 12 HOT CROSS BUNS (OR 18 MINIS)
THE BUNS
1 cup (250 ml) milk and water (about half and half)
½ cup (100 g) sugar (superfine granulated or light brown)
1 package active dry yeast
4 ounces (100 g) golden raisins
1 pound (450 g) white bread flour, or whole wheat flour
½ teaspoon mixed spice
½ teaspoon cinnamon
½ teaspoon nutmeg
1 stick (8 tablespoons) (113 g) butter or margarine
1 egg, beaten

THE CROSSES
4 ounces (100 g) white bread flour
½ stick (4 tablespoons) (113 g) butter or margarine
1–2 tablespoons water

THE GLAZE
4 tablespoons water
4 tablespoons sugar

## FOR THE BUNS

1. Gently heat the milk and water in a saucepan (don't let it boil). Once its warm, stir in the sugar, then sprinkle the dried yeast on top and let proof for about 10 minutes while you wash the raisins in warm water. (Dry the raisins in an old, clean tea towel.)

2. Sift the flour and spices into a large mixing bowl and rub in the butter until the mixture resembles medium-fine bread crumbs.

3. Make a well in the center, add the beaten egg and warm milk and mix everything together with a fork to make a firm dough.

4. Turn the dough out onto a floured surface and knead for about 5 minutes, then leave to proof for about 10 minutes *(see Note below)*.

5. Place the dough on a floured surface and knead again for a couple of minutes, then shape into rolls—about the size of a satsuma—flatten them slightly and place on the greased baking sheet. (You might want to use 2 baking sheets so you can spread the buns out a bit more.)

6. Lightly score a cross on top of each bun with the side of a knife and proof for 10 minutes more.

## FOR THE CROSSES

1. While the buns are proofing, rub in the butter and flour and mix to a firm dough with the water, then turn the dough out onto a floured surface. Roll it out as thinly as you can without breaking, and cut it into long, thin strips with a sharp knife.

2. Dunk the strips into a cup of cold milk and water and stick them to the buns where you marked out the crosses, then using your fingers or a pastry brush, lightly glaze all the buns with the milk and water.

3. Bake in the oven, preheated to 350°F (180°C) for about 20 minutes, until the buns are a light, golden brown.

FOR THE GLAZE
1. While the buns are in the oven, heat the water and sugar in a deep-sided saucepan until the sugar is dissolved, then allow to boil for a few minutes to make a fairly thin syrup.
2. Take the buns from the oven and while they're still warm, brush them with the syrup and leave to cool.

Note: *You need to prove the dough in a warm place—the airing cupboard is ideal—in which case you can wrap the dough in plastic wrap. Otherwise, use your oven on the lowest possible setting, putting the dough on a greased baking sheet—the one you're going to use for baking the buns will do—and covering with a clean, damp tea towel.*

## Honeycomb

Use a very large saucepan and don't worry about the shocking state of the pan afterwards; it only needs a 5-minute soak in very hot water and, hey presto, it's clean again.

8 heaping tablespoons sugar
8 heaping tablespoons golden syrup
4 tablespoons water
4 rounded teaspoons baking soda

1. Lightly oil a sheet of wax paper and put it in a shallow bowl, plate, or cake pan.
2. Put the sugar, golden syrup, and water in a large saucepan over a moderate heat, mix it all together, and stir continuously with a wooden spoon.

3. Let the syrup boil for up to 5 minutes—keep your eye on the clock—by which time it should be a rich, golden brown (but not too dark, you don't want it burned).
4. Quickly add the baking soda, still stirring rapidly, and remove the pan from the heat as soon as the honeycomb froths and rises up in the pan.
5. Scrape the honeycomb onto the wax paper immediately and let set for about 1 hour before breaking it up into chunks.

## Ginger Beer

I first made ginger beer in primary school with the same teacher who taught us to make miniature pancakes on top of an old baked bean can with a candle underneath. (Mrs Jones, where are you now? And can you imagine what the health and safety brigade would say about candles in the classroom today?)

Anyway, I remember being bitterly disappointed after all the waiting, never having tried ginger beer before, and thinking it tasted revolting. Now I like it, and this process is so straightforward it's a good project for kids to have a go at during those long school holidays—or you can start on a Saturday and finish it off the following weekend.

Like other beer and ciders, ginger beer can also be used in cooking (*see Ginger Beer Pork, page 62*).

TO START:
½ cup (125 ml) fresh, cold water
1 tablespoon ground ginger
1 heaping teaspoon light brown sugar

1. Put the cold water, ginger, and sugar in a clean, dry jar with a tight-fitting lid, and give it a good shake.
2. Every day for the next *7 days* add 1 heaping teaspoon of ginger

and 1 level teaspoon of sugar to the jar; then holding the jar by the lid, gently swish round for a few seconds before leaving it to stand.

THE GINGER BEER (LEAVE FOR AT LEAST 12 HOURS AFTER THE FINAL ADDITION OF SUGAR AND GINGER)
2 liter bottles (2 quarts each) bottled spring water
2 lemons
3 cups boiling water
1 level teaspoon active dry yeast
1½ cups (265 g) light brown sugar

1. Fill (or half-fill) the kettle with water from one of the 2-quart bottles of mineral water.
2. Using an old, clean tea towel, carefully strain the ginger and sugar mixture from the jar through the cloth, into a very large mixing bowl. If the tea towel is very old and threadbare, fold it in half so as not to let too much of the sediment through.
3. Squeeze both lemons through a clean part of the cloth—squeezing the cloth gently with your fingers to let as much juice into the bowl as you can.
4. Pour three mugs of boiling water into the bowl and add the yeast and sugar, stirring for a couple of minutes until all the sugar has dissolved.
5. Allow the liquid to stand for half an hour, then strain through another old, clean tea towel (or thoroughly rinse the first one and use it again; doesn't matter if it's damp) and add the entire contents of the second bottle of water, plus whatever remains from the first bottle, and mix well.
6. Use a jug or funnel to pour the ginger beer into the two bottles (adding the whisky if you're using it) and refrigerate. As soon

as the ginger beer is chilled, it's ready to drink. If you find there's still a lot of sediment in the bottle after 24 hours, strain the ginger beer through an old, clean tea towel again, rinse out the bottle, and pour the drink back in.

Note: *To make an alcoholic version, add a double measure of whisky (2 × 35 ml) — or a miniature—to a 2-quart bottle of ginger beer at the final stage.*

## Toffee Apples

The amounts given here are enough for eight toffee apples but it's a good idea to make a greater quantity of caramel than you need so you've got more to play around with; the syrup thickens very rapidly as it cools, which makes it trickier to get a nice, even layer of caramel over the last few apples.

MAKES 8 TOFFEE APPLES
8 apples
1¾ (300 g) light brown or superfine granulated sugar
½ stick (4 tablespoons) (56 g) butter
¼ cup plus 1 tablespoon (100 g) golden syrup
1 teaspoon lemon juice
½ cup (125 ml) water
Lollipop sticks

1. Lightly grease a large sheet of wax paper and have a large bowl of cold water ready beside the stove.
2. Wash the apples in lukewarm water and dry them thoroughly, then push a wooden stick into each one, where the stem used to be, about halfway through.
3. Put all the ingredients for the caramel into a large saucepan

and stir over a low heat for a few minutes until the sugar has completely dissolved.

4. Increase the heat to medium-high and allow the syrup to boil fairly rapidly for about 15 minutes, stirring occasionally.

5. After 20 minutes (not a minute more with this quantity) drop about half a teaspoon of the boiling syrup into the cold water; if it hardens immediately it's ready. A fudgier sort of caramel means it needs to be boiled a little longer—coat the apples with too-soft caramel and you'll never get it off your teeth.

6. *Test again after 1 minute.*

7. When the caramel is ready, take the pan off the heat and tilt it slightly, making it easier to dip the apples.

8. Swirl the apples around in the syrup one at a time, as quickly as you can, then plunge them straight into the bowl of cold water and then set them upside down on the wax paper to dry completely.

## BOTTLING IT

For chutney, fruit spread, and grapefruit curd (see below) the jars always need to be warm—regardless of whether the produce is going in hot or cold—in order to prevent mildew forming. You can warm the jars by rinsing them in very hot water and drying them quickly, but an easier way is to put the jars in the microwave; about 45 seconds (or 1 minute) on high should do it.

### Chutney

This is great as a dip, or with cheese, baked potatoes, and cold meats, or try adding a couple of spoonfuls to curry, pasta sauce, and nut roasts for extra flavor.

You should get about six standard-size jam jars out of this recipe, so if you want to make less, halve the quantities.

1 pound golden raisins
1 head celery
2 onions
2 cups (500 ml) brown (or white) malt vinegar
1 cup (250 ml) water
1 level tablespoon salt
2⅔ tablespoons sugar (350 g) Demerara sugar
1 heaping teaspoon mixed spice
5–6 large cooking apples

1. Wash the raisins in warm water.
2. Cut off the top and root ends of the celery and remove the leaves. Peel the onions, then roughly chop all the vegetables into small chunks. (Leave the apples until the end to keep them going brown.)
3. Pour the vinegar and water into a large saucepan and add the chopped vegetables, golden raisins, salt, sugar, and spice.
4. Cut the apples into quarters (or even smaller), peel, core, cut into small chunks and add to the pan.
5. Give everything a good stir and bring to the boil over a moderate heat, then turn the heat right down and simmer very gently for 1½– 2 hours, stirring occasionally.
6. When the chutney looks ready—it will be thick, pulpy, and sweet smelling—pour it into a large bowl, cover with an old, clean tea towel, and let stand for at least a few hours, and preferably overnight.
7. Bottle in warm, dry jars (*see above*) and store in the pantry.

## Soft Fruit Spread

Jam making for absolute beginners; this is as easy as it gets, but because it doesn't keep quite as well as regular jam, which is made with twice the amount of sugar. Store it in the fridge and use within a couple of weeks once the jar is opened.

Any soft fruit, or a mixture of soft fruits will do, such as raspberries, blackberries, black currants, red currants, and cherries. If you get the chance to pick blackberries for free at the end of August/beginning of September, make the most of it; they freeze well and you can do lots with them.

You should get a couple of jars from this amount of fruit and sugar, so increase the quantities and use a larger pan if you want to make more.

2 pounds (1 kg) soft fruit
1 pound (450 g) granulated sugar
2 lemons

1. Put the fruit in a saucepan with the sugar, juice from both lemons, and a little water—unless the fruit is already very wet and running with juice, in which case you may not need any. *Heat very gently for a few minutes*, stirring often with a wooden spoon, to give the sugar time to dissolve.
2. Increase the heat and boil fairly rapidly for 20–30 minutes until the jam thickens and gels and it separates in the saucepan for a couple of seconds when you run the wooden spoon through the middle.
3. Remove the jam from the heat and let it stand for about 10 minutes, then pour it into warm, dry jars.
4. Leave to cool for another 10 minutes, then cover. Refrigerate.

## Grapefruit Curd

Homemade fruit curd is similar to store-bought, but less solid, with a purer taste and texture. If you'd rather have a thicker, jelly-like curd, add a teaspoon of cornstarch mixed with a table-spoonful of water and a few drops of lemon juice at the end; thick or thin, it's equally good on bread and crackers or as a fill-ing in cakes and pastries. To make lemon curd, just use 2 lemons (rind and juice) instead of one grapefruit.

MAKES ROUGHLY 1 STANDARD-SIZE JAM JAR
5 tablespoons plus 1 teaspoon (75 g) butter
1 cup plus 2 tablespoons (225 g) superfine granulated sugar
1 grapefruit, grated rind and juice
3 eggs, beaten

1. Melt the butter in a saucepan over moderate heat.
2. Add the sugar with the finely grated rind and juice of the grapefruit and stir for a couple of minutes until all the sugar has dissolved.
3. Pour in the beaten egg and stir briskly and continuously with a wooden spoon to prevent the egg separating while the mix-ture thickens. (Don't panic if any little white flecks of egg do develop; you can get rid of these when you strain the curd at the end.)
4. After about 10 minutes the curd should have reached the consistency of custard, which means it's ready.
5. Strain through a sieve into a measuring cup and pour straight into the warm jar. Leave to cool for about 30 minutes, then put the lid on and store it in the fridge.

## Figgy Pudding

I've always liked the idea of Christmas pudding made with figs as the song suggests but by far the best thing about this pudding, apart from the short list of ingredients, is the fact that it doesn't need time to mature, meaning you can make it a couple of days before Christmas. On the other hand it keeps really well too, so make two and save one for next year.

The quantities here make three 1-pound puddings, so if you only want one large pudding to get you and your family through Christmas, halve all the measurements except for the sherry and make one big pudding in a 1½–2-pound pudding basin, in which case you should steam it for the maximum four hours.

Cover each pudding with a double thickness of wax paper with a pleat in the middle to allow for any expansion, then put a layer of aluminium foil over the top of the wax paper, also with a pleat in the middle, and fold the foil tightly around the rim, or secure with string.

Finally, if you want to put a coin in for good luck (£1 must be the going rate these days), wrap it in aluminium foil and pop it in before covering the pudding for the first time.

MAKE THREE 1-POUND PUDDINGS
THE PUDDINGS
1 pound (400–500 g) white bread crumbs (5–6 cups)
2 oz (50 g) self-rising flour
4 ounces (100 g) suet
½ cup plus 1 tablespoon (100 g) light brown sugar
½ teaspoon salt
3 teaspoons mixed spice
1 pound dried figs

1 pound mixed fruit
¼ cup (25 g) flaked almonds
½ cup (125 ml) sherry or brandy
⅓ cup (90 ml) milk
2 eggs, beaten

THE BRANDY BUTTER
5 tablespoons plus 1 teaspoon (75 g) unsalted butter
½ cup plus 2 tablespoons (75 g) confectioners' sugar
2 tablespoons brandy (or sherry or whisky)

FOR THE PUDDINGS
1. Grease the pudding basins with butter.
2. Mix the bread crumbs with the sifted flour, suet, sugar, salt, and spices in a very large mixing bowl.
3. Wash the mixed fruit in warm water, dry thoroughly in an old, clean tea towel, and chop the figs into small pieces (wash them too, unless the packaging states "ready to eat").
4. Crumble up the flaked almonds with your hands and add them to the bowl with the fruit, followed by the sherry, milk, and beaten eggs.
5. Stir thoroughly for 1 minute, making sure everything is combined, then put the mixture into the prepared pudding basins, cover, and let stand overnight.
6. Cover puddings with wax paper and foil. Steam the puddings for 3–4 hours (depending on size) in a saucepan of boiling water, topping up the level of water every now and then to prevent the saucepan from boiling dry.
7. After steaming, allow the puddings to cool for at least 1 hour before removing the foil and wax paper and covering with wax paper and fresh foil.

8. Store the puddings at room temperature and steam again for 2 more hours just before serving with brandy butter, custard, or cream.

### FOR THE BRANDY BUTTER

1. Bring the butter to room temperature, then beat it in a mixing bowl with an electric hand mixer until it's light and fluffy—or use a wooden spoon, if you've got enough strength left in your arm (it's Christmas, remember).
2. Gradually beat in the confectioners' sugar, followed by the brandy or other spirit, and chill in the fridge for an hour before serving.

## Fudge

There's something upscale and sophisticated about fudge compared with your average chewy toffee, but although it gives the impression that it's been made with great skill by a very clever cook, all you need to do is spend a few minutes stirring butter, sugar, and milk together while you think about something more important. Just like the Honey, Lemon & Yogurt Cake (page 196), any kind of homemade fudge—chocolate, coffee, fruity, extra creamy, coconut—not only looks good, it has the magical effect of making the person who made it look good too. Result.

The quantities given here make 36 good-size squares in an 8-inch (21 cm) square cake pan, or similar, but if you haven't made fudge before and are a bit unsure, you may want to make only half this amount, in which case you shouldn't need to boil the mixture for any longer than 15 minutes (start testing after 10 minutes).

Once you've taken the fudge off the heat it's better to cool it down quickly rather than beating it by hand for at least another

10 minutes while you stand around wondering if it's going to work, so place the pan in a shallow bowl of cold water or, if you can bear to get another pan dirty, scrape the fudge into a clean, cool one. After a couple of minutes the fudge will start to thicken and lose its shine, becoming dull and slightly grainy—exactly how you'd expect fudge to look—then all you have to do is add the flavoring and get it into the pan.

MAKES 36 SQUARES
12½ tablespoons (175 g) unsalted butter
1¾ cups plus 2 tablespoons (410 g) evaporated milk
About ½ cup (125 ml) milk
2 pounds (1 kg) sugar

1. Melt the butter in a large saucepan while you lightly grease and long-strip-line a square or rectangular cake pan.
2. Pour the evaporated milk into a large measuring cup then top up to the 2 cup (500 ml) mark with the milk.
3. Add the milk and sugar to the pan over a low heat and leave it for about 5 minutes, stirring occasionally, until the sugar has dissolved.
4. Bring to the boil, then boil rapidly for 15–20 minutes, stirring continuously, until the syrup reaches the soft ball stage, meaning ½ teaspoon of syrup dropped into a cup of cold water holds its shape and looks and feels like a piece of soft toffee when you squeeze it.
5. Remove the pan from the heat and allow the fudge to cool for a few minutes *(see above)*, beating almost constantly, then add the flavoring and scrape the fudge into the prepared pan.
6. Mark the fudge into squares after about 15 minutes; leave it in the pan for at least 2 hours to cool completely, then lift it out, cut it up, and store in an airtight container.

ALSO TRY . . .

Coffee & Vanilla Fudge.

1 teaspoon instant coffee, dissolved in 1 tablespoon boiling water
2 teaspoons vanilla extract

While the fudge is cooling, quickly dissolve 1 teaspoon of instant coffee in a cup with 1 teaspoon of boiling water, then mix with the vanilla extract and thoroughly beat the liquid into the fudge.

Chocolate Marble Fudge
3 ounces (75 g) plain dark chocolate

1. Break the chocolate into pieces and melt in a bowl over a saucepan of boiling water while you make the fudge.
2. As soon as the fudge is cool and ready to go into the pan, pour the chocolate into the middle of the fudge and stir *only once or twice* in clean, sweeping movements, to create a marbled effect. Pour the fudge into the pan and leave to set.

"The most remarkable thing about my mother is that for thirty years she served the family nothing but leftovers. The original meal has never been found."

—Calvin Trillin

# 10

# Weekly menu planning

*It's not only desperate housewives who plan a week's worth of evening meals in advance, so don't be put off if you haven't tried this before. Go shopping with a list and you're far less likely to waste time wandering up and down the aisles, absent-mindedly loading up your cart with random items.*

There can't be many people who've never gone to the supermarket for a loaf of bread and come out half an hour later with three grocery bags full of impulse buys. There's been a series of surveys in recent years claiming that in Britain we waste billions of pounds a year on food, much of which gets chucked away while it's still perfectly edible (whatever the sell-by date says), mainly because we buy whatever takes our fancy at the time without thinking about when and how we're going to use it.

Such is the seductive power of the supermarket.

If, like me, you struggle with portion control—meaning your dinners for four people could easily feed six—a menu plan could also help you get your worst excesses under control. The other thing I like about planning meals in advance is, contrary to what you might expect, it completely takes the focus away from food, so once you've worked out the menu for the week and done the shopping you can just forget all about it.

And if lack of inspiration is your biggest problem, you'll find a few minutes of planning means you can go for weeks without eating the same dinner twice.

Another benefit is the rollover effect. Make a greater quantity of food for the same amount of effort then use what's left over to make a completely hassle-free meal the next day.

Best of all, not only does a plan save time, it can also save you a lot of money.

The food for the menus in this chapter was purchased in five different supermarkets, and although the price and quality of some of the items varies, it's still possible to spend around thirty pounds (or less) on family dinners for one working week, i.e., Monday to Friday—with a bit left over.

Of course you also need to buy laundry detergent and tooth-paste, not to mention food for breakfast, lunch, and snacks, but most household items last longer than a week anyway, and if you keep plenty of nonperishable items in stock you should find you only need to buy the fresh ingredients on a weekly basis.

Still on the subject of saving money, I'd rather buy store-brand toiletries and the cheapest chips, crackers or cookies, and trash-can liners, dishwashing liquid, and so on, and spend more money where it matters, on good, cheaper cuts of meat, chicken, eggs, or-ganic milk, and fresh vegetables. All supermarkets love misleading shoppers with "specials" to get you hooked on something before they raise the prices but it's up to you to make this strategy work in your favor by taking advantage of a good buy, and moving on to an-other brand, as soon as something becomes too expensive.

Remember how many rival supermarkets there are now, and how much choice is available. It's well-known, too, that some are quite a lot cheaper than others, so it figures that you can save a considerable amount of money just by changing your shopping habits.

That said, one of the drawbacks with the cheaper supermar-kets is the limited choice of certain items; also the fact that they don't always stock everything you want from one week to the next, which is pretty annoying, especially when you can't get hold of a basic, everyday food that you should be able to take for granted.

On the other hand, how much choice do you really need when you only want one type of canned fruit in the first place? Isn't it worth making a few minor adjustments to your food shopping when you can guarantee a much smaller bill at the end? Or maybe you'd rather spend more money and save yourself the hassle of deciding what else to buy when you have to cross the omelette off the menu because the supermarket has run out of eggs.

I know people who actually spread their grocery shopping across two or three different supermarkets *every single week*, but I can't see this working if you have a job as well as a family, or you just hate shopping—or all three. As far as I'm concerned, the less time spent in the supermarket the better, which is why I tend to go to one of the budget supermarkets when I'm stocking up on basics, and a big-name store when I want mostly fresh food and need to be sure I'll find exactly what I'm looking for.

Finally, even if you don't have to stick to a budget, there's something very liberating about saving money on groceries and having more disposable income left to spend on really important things, like lipstick!

## THE MENUS

**WEEK 1**

| Monday: | Chili Con Carne & Rice |
| Tuesday: | Chili & Chips |
| Wednesday: | Veggie Burgers & Potato Wedges |
| Thursday: | Chinese Chicken Stir-fry |
| Friday: | Hot Dogs & DIY Pasta Sauce |

WEEK 2

| | |
|---|---|
| Monday: | Roast Chicken |
| Tuesday: | Chicken & Leek Casserole |
| Wednesday: | Bubble, Bangers & Beans |
| Thursday: | Kedgeree |
| Friday: | Cheese & Spinach Omelette |

WEEK 3

| | |
|---|---|
| Monday: | Boiled Bacon & Roasted Vegetables |
| Tuesday: | Vegetable Tortilla |
| Wednesday: | Meatballs, Tagliatelle & Tomato Sauce |
| Thursday: | Stuffed Peppers |
| Friday: | Pacific Pie |

WEEK 4

| | |
|---|---|
| Monday: | Liver (or Bratwurst) Bacon & Onions |
| Tuesday: | Tomato & Red Lentil Soup |
| Wednesday: | Salmon & Tomato Pasta Bake |
| Thursday: | Pork Loin Steaks, Sausages & Rice |
| Friday: | Bread-Roll-Pizzas |

WEEK 5

| | |
|---|---|
| Monday: | Corned Beef Hash |
| Tuesday: | Fishstick Pie |
| Wednesday: | Spaghetti Bolognese |
| Thursday: | Curried Nut Roast |
| Friday: | Bacon, Egg & Homemade Fries |

# WEEK ONE

| | |
|---|---|
| MONDAY: | Chili Con Carne |
| TUESDAY: | Chili & Chips |
| WEDNESDAY: | Veggie Burgers & Potato Wedges |
| THURSDAY: | Chinese Chicken Stir-fry |
| FRIDAY: | Hotdogs & DIY Pasta Sauce |

## THE SHOPPING LIST

- Ground beef
- Chicken portions
- Hotdogs
- Kidney beans
- Chickpeas
- Mozzarella cheese
- Penne pasta
- Long-grain rice
- Mushrooms
- Chinese stir-fry vegetables
- Potatoes
- Avocados
- Spinach
- Tomatoes
- Carrots
- Broccoli
- Onions
- Zucchini
- Bell peppers (mixed colors)
- Noodles (Asian and egg)
- Oatmeal
- Whole wheat flour
- Tomato paste
- Eggs (12 free-range)
- Tortilla chips

# WEEK ONE: THE RECIPES

MONDAY:
CHILI CON CARNE & RICE (page 43).

TUESDAY:
CHILI & CHIPS
I always buy the cheapest supermarket store-brand plain tortilla chips, because they contain less salt and are completely free from artificial coloring and flavorings, none of which you need anyway when you've got chili.

Remains of yesterday's chili
2 bags tortilla chips
Grated cheddar or mozzarella cheese
Avocado
Tomatoes (at least one per person)

1.  Reheat the chili in a large ovenproof dish covered with aluminium foil (or a lid) in a 350°F (180°C) oven for about 20 minutes until the chili is piping hot. Alternatively, cover with a lid and reheat in the microwave on high for about 5 minutes, giving the chili a good stir halfway through.
2.  Empty a packet of tortilla chips over the chili, mix them up a bit with the meaty sauce, then sprinkle liberally with grated cheese and return to the oven or flash under the broiler for a couple of minutes so the cheese melts and the edges of the tortilla chips on the top brown ever so slightly. (Don't let them burn.)
3.  Serve with chunks of avocado and tomato wedges.

WEDNESDAY:
VEGGIE BURGERS & POTATO WEDGES (page 79).
Approximately 3–4 small potatoes per person

THE POTATO WEDGES

1. Wash the potatoes with a vegetable brush in a bowl of cold water and cut each one lengthwise into sixths or eighths, depending on size.
2. Preheat the oil, or whatever fat you're using, in a large oven-proof dish, pop the wedges in, sprinkle with paprika, baste with the hot oil and bake for about half an hour until they're as brown and crisp as you like them, basting them again with the peppery oil about halfway through the baking time.
3. Serve with corn and something green; French beans, curly kale, or broccoli, for example.

THURSDAY:
CHINESE CHICKEN STIR-FRY
When making a stir-fry, make sure the meat's cooked through before you add the vegetables and noodles.

FRIDAY:
FRANKFURTERS & DIY PASTA SAUCE
This is just a variation of the recipe for DIY Pasta Sauce (page 93). (There can't be much nutritional value in a frankfurter, but does it really matter when they taste this good and you've got all the vegetables you need in the pasta sauce?)

# WEEK TWO

| | |
|---|---|
| MONDAY: | Roast Chicken |
| TUESDAY: | Chicken & Leek Casserole |
| WEDNESDAY: | Bubble, Bangers & Beans |
| THURSDAY: | Kedgeree |
| FRIDAY: | Cheese & Spinach Omelette |

THE SHOPPING LIST:

- 1 chicken
- Chipolata sausages (3 packs × 12: 82 percent pork)
- Smoked mackerel
- Cheese
- Eggs (12 free range)
- Milk
- 1 can condensed chicken soup
- Brown rice
- Baked beans in tomato sauce
- Plum tomatoes
- Oven fries
- Potatoes
- Frozen peas
- Carrots
- Spinach
- Leeks
- Broccoli
- Parsnips
- White cabbage

# WEEK TWO: THE RECIPES

MONDAY:

ROAST CHICKEN WITH ROAST POTATOES AND PARSNIPS, WHITE CABBAGE, CARROTS, AND PEAS.

With plenty of vegetables, one large chicken should be enough to make a meal for four people two nights running, so try not to scoff down the whole thing in one sitting. But having just said that, you won't necessarily get as much chicken as you want for Monday's roast if you like a lot of meat, so you could also have some of the chipolatas with this dinner to bulk it out a bit more. Even if you're feeding six people, you won't need all 36 chipolatas for Wednesday's dinner. (And don't forget to use the chicken carcass to make stock; you can always keep the stock in the freezer until you need it.)

If you're out all day you'll probably have to roast your chicken on Sunday night, in which case be careful not to overcook it or the chicken will be dry when you warm it up again. Once cooked, as soon as the chicken is cool enough to handle, carve the meat off and divide it into two casserole dishes, cover them with lids or aluminium foil, and store both in the fridge for Monday and Tuesday.

SHOPPING LIST
Roast chicken
Potatoes
Rosemary
Parsnips
White cabbage
Peas
Carrots

1. Peel the potatoes and parboil for a few minutes while you heat the fat in the oven (*see Tips, page 92*) then sprinkle with rosemary.
2. Cut the parsnips into small wedges and roast them alongside the potatoes.
3. Save one-fourth of the cabbage to make coleslaw with at the end of the week if you like, otherwise cook the whole thing; there should plenty left over to make Bubble & Squeak on Wednesday. Store cooked leftover cabbage, peas, and carrots in the fridge, keeping them well covered.

TUESDAY:
CHICKEN & LEEK CASSEROLE
The word *casserole* is a bit of an exaggeration for something as basic as this, but it looks and tastes a bit like a casserole, and I don't know what else to call it.

Potatoes
Remains of yesterday's chicken
Oil
Butter
Tarragon
2 leeks
Spinach
1 can condensed soup (chicken or mushroom)
Milk
Peas

1.  Peel potatoes (enough for tonight's dinner and tomorrow's Bubble & Squeak) and boil in a large saucepan of cold water.
2.  Cut the chicken into chunks or small pieces, sauté gently in a little oil and butter in another large saucepan, adding the tarragon or whatever herbs you want to use, if any.
3.  Thoroughly wash and finely chop the leeks and spinach and put them in the pan with the chicken; add the condensed soup, stir well and thin the soup down with a little milk until it reaches the consistency you want. Don't let the soup boil. Cover the casserole with a lid and simmer gently until the potatoes are cooked. (Transfer the casserole to an ovenproof dish and keep warm in the oven if you prefer.)
4.  Meanwhile, cook the frozen peas in boiling water for a few minutes while you mash the potatoes, then serve.

WEDNESDAY:
BUBBLE, BANGERS & BEANS
Traditionally, the British dish, Bubble & Squeak was made from leftover potatoes, cabbage, and onions mashed up together and fried in dripping, but use whatever combination of leftover vegetables you like; broccoli, peas and carrots, curly kale, Brussels

sprouts . . . it doesn't really matter. As long as you've got plenty of potatoes in there, anything goes.

1. Cook the sausages in the oven; it's less messy and you don't need any extra oil or fat.
2. Fry your "Bubble" in the biggest pan you've got and preheat the oil or lard until it's practically smoking. Alternatively, put it in a buttered ovenproof dish, dotting the top all over with butter.
3. To save time and energy, warm the baked beans up in the oven, rather than use another saucepan or put them in the microwave—there's no point when you've got all that heat going on already. Put the beans in a Pyrex dish on the bottom shelf or on the oven floor 10 minutes before the end of cooking time and give them a good stir when you take them out.

THURSDAY:
KEDGEREE (page 73).

FRIDAY:
CHEESE & SPINACH OMELETTE (WITH OVEN FRIES)
Classic omelettes are made individually with three eggs per person (more cholesterol anyone?) by clever chefs who whisk and flip everything around in the pan until somehow they've produced a perfect, cigar-shaped omelette; firm on the outside, soft and still slightly runny on the inside. But the other, much easier way of making omelettes means you can get away with using just one egg per person (if that's all you've got) as long as there's plenty of filling.

If you've got the time and the inclination (it's Friday, remember), make coleslaw by finely shredding a bit of the leftover raw cabbage with some thinly sliced carrots and onion then adding a couple of spoonfuls of mayonnaise, or a mixture of mayonnaise and natural yogurt. If you're having oven fries, put them in first and make the omelette—which only takes about ten minutes from start to finish—once the fries are almost done.

SERVES 4
Cheddar cheese
Spinach
Eggs (4–6)
Salt and pepper
Butter

1.  Grate the cheese, wash the spinach and tear it into small pieces, whisk the eggs with a fork and add a splash of cold water. Season with salt and pepper.
2.  Warm the butter in a large frying pan, pour the eggs in, add the spinach and cheese and fluff the whole thing with a fork until it's all mixed up and the spinach is submerged.
3.  Leave the omelette to set over a very low heat for a few minutes then put it under the grill for another couple of minutes until the top of the omelette sets and rises and turns golden.

# WEEK THREE

Because there were no single cans of baked beans in the supermarket, only multi-packs of four, I opted for a can of spaghetti hoops instead. (Never again though ... enough said.) There was no ground pork either, so I bought ground beef for Wednesday's meatballs.

| MONDAY: | Boiled Bacon & Roasted Vegetables |
|---|---|
| TUESDAY: | Vegetable Tortilla |
| WEDNESDAY: | Meatballs, Tagliatelle & Tomato Sauce |
| THURSDAY: | Stuffed Peppers |
| FRIDAY: | Pacific Pie |

THE SHOPPING LIST:

- Gammon joint (mildly cured pork, ham)
- Tuna (2 small cans)

- Cheese
- Chopped tomatoes
- Plum tomatoes
- Spaghetti hoops
- Ground beef
- Whole kernel corn
- Green beans

- Mixed bell peppers
- Potatoes
- Savoy cabbage
- Couscous
- Mushrooms
- Butternut squash
- Tagliatelle
- Tortellini (2 packages)
- Onions
- Chips

# WEEK THREE: THE RECIPES

MONDAY:

## BOILED BACON & ROAST POTATOES WITH ROASTED VEGETABLES

The bacon joint can be roasted or boiled (ahead of time if you're out all day), then sliced up and reheated at the bottom of the oven halfway through the vegetables' cooking time. (If you've got more bacon than you want to use tonight, save some for tomorrow.)

Make more roasted vegetables than you need and keep the rest in the fridge for Tuesday's vegetable tortilla. The quantities below should be more than enough for four people with plenty left over, especially if you're having roast potatoes and more green vegetables. And if in doubt, my advice would always be to just make more.

ROASTED VEGETABLES
4 medium potatoes
1 butternut squash
4–5 large carrots
3 bell peppers: red, yellow, orange (preferably one of each)
2 onions
Mushrooms
Olive oil
Sesame seeds

GRAVY
Instant gravy granules
Tomato paste
1 cup (250 ml) boiling water

1. Peel potatoes first so you can parboil them on a low heat while you prepare the rest of the vegetables, then roast them separately on a higher shelf and swap them over with the vegetables about halfway through.
2. Cut the butternut squash in half; peel the skin with a potato peeler, remove the seeds and the foamy inner bit and cut into wedges.
3. Scrape the carrots and slice diagonally (long thin carrots are best for this). Halve the peppers and cut them into strips; peel and slice the onions, or if you're using shallots, peel and cut them into halves or quarters; cut the mushrooms into chunks.

4. Put the vegetables into a large ovenproof dish, drizzle with olive oil, and sprinkle with sesame seeds and roast in the oven preheated to 400°F (200°C) for 20–30 minutes.

5. In a measuring cup mix 1 tablespoon of gravy granules with a little tomato paste, add boiling water up to the 1 cup mark and whisk with a fork. Pour the gravy over the bacon in an ovenproof dish, cover with a lid or a piece of aluminium foil, and put in the bottom of the preheated oven until the roast potatoes and vegetables are done. (Or if you prefer, reheat the bacon in the microwave.)

TUESDAY:
VEGETABLE TORTILLA
Not strictly a vegetable tortilla if you're adding leftover bacon, obviously . . .

Oil
2 tablespoons all-purpose flour
1 egg
1 cup (250 ml) milk
Remains of yesterday's roasted vegetables
Leftover bacon

1. Preheat the oven to 400–425°F (200–220°C), and warm a little oil in a very large ovenproof dish.

2. Make a thin pancake batter with the flour, egg, and milk, then mash the leftover roasted vegetables with a fork. Beat the vegetable mash together with the batter to make a kind of paste.

3. If you've got leftover bacon, chop it into small pieces and put it into the hot oil first, then spread the veggie batter mix over the top to completely cover the bottom of the dish.

4. The tortilla cooks in about 20 minutes so if you want baked beans and canned plum tomatoes with it, put them in a covered casserole dish at the very bottom of the oven at the same time.

WEDNESDAY:
MEATBALLS WITH TAGLIATELLE & TOMATO SAUCE *(see DIY Pasta Sauce, page 93)*.
For an even quicker alternative to the DIY Pasta Sauce, make the easy tomato sauce below:

1 onion, or a few shallots
Spinach
Olive oil
Butter
1 can chopped tomatoes
Herbs: Basil, Italian herbs, or parsley
Tomato paste
Garlic paste

1. Chop the onion or shallots. Wash and tear spinach into small pieces.
2. Warm the oil and butter in a large shallow pan; add the onion and spinach and fry for a few minutes until the onion is soft.
3. Add the canned tomatoes, increase the heat until it sizzles, then add the herbs, tomato and garlic pastes, and stir well. Reduce the heat simmer the sauce until the pasta is ready.

THURSDAY:
STUFFED PEPPERS (page 77).

Friday:
Pacific Pie (*page 100*).

# WEEK FOUR

Different budget supermarket, same problem with very limited range of stock. There was no liver at all, so I bought two packets of Bratwurst sausages instead, which were actually quite good and contained a minimum of 86 percent pork. Bratwursts are also extra large and unlike some other sausages they don't shrink once they're cooked, in which case one would be enough for some people, especially children. (The downside is having sausages twice in the same week.)

Nor were there any lentils in this supermarket, and I couldn't find anything remotely similar—dried chickpeas, beans, or other pulses—which doesn't matter if you already have some in the pantry at home, but still, it's something to watch out for. (In other words, if you're following this week's menu plan and you're sure you want liver, shop at one of the other supermarkets.)

| | |
|---|---|
| Monday: | Liver (or Bratwurst Sausages) |
| | Bacon & Onions |
| Tuesday: | Tomato & Red Lentil Soup |
| Wednesday: | Salmon & Tomato Pasta Bake |
| Thursday: | Pork Loin Steaks, Sausages & Rice |
| Friday: | Bread Roll Pizzas |

The Shopping List:
- Back bacon, or Irish bacon (2 packages)
- Bratwurst sausages (2 × 6)
- Pork loin chops
- Salmon (2 small cans)
- Oranges

- Rice
- Pasta
- Soft bread rolls
  (2×6)
- Cheese
- Broccoli
- Onions

- Mushrooms
- Spinach
- Potatoes
- Fresh tomatoes
- Cucumber
- Plum tomatoes (2 cans)
- Pineapple slices

# WEEK FOUR: THE RECIPES

MONDAY:
LIVER (OR BRATWURST SAUSAGES) BACON, & ONIONS with
mashed potatoes and green vegetables

Potatoes (for however much mash you want)
1–2 packets of liver (or 1 packet of 6 large Bratwurst sausages)
Flour seasoned with salt and pepper
Oil
2 onions
1 cup lamb or beef stock
Tomato paste
1 package bacon (regular or back), or substitute Irish bacon

1.  Peel the potatoes and put them on to simmer gently while
    you prepare the liver in the usual way; wash it well, remove
    any sinewy bits, and coat in a little seasoned flour. (If you've
    bought Bratwurst sausages, cook them according to the in-
    structions on the package; they take 20–25 minutes in a
    moderate oven.) Otherwise, warm some oil in a large pan and

fry the liver for a couple of minutes before transferring to a casserole dish with a lid.

2. Fry the onions the way you like them and add the stock to the pan with a big spoonful of tomato paste; stir well, then pour the onion gravy into the casserole dish and put it in the middle of a moderate oven.

3. Roll up the bacon slices and place on a baking tray on the top shelf of the oven.

4. When the bacon rolls are brown and crisp, 20–25 minutes, slice thinly, and scatter over the liver and onions. Serve with mashed potatoes and green vegetables.

TUESDAY:
TOMATO & RED LENTIL SOUP (page 119).
Cheese on toast or bacon sandwiches are perfect with tomato soup.

WEDNESDAY:
SALMON & TOMATO PASTA BAKE
Needless to say, this can just as easily be made with canned tuna instead of salmon.

Tomato & Red Lentil Soup (or any other fresh or frozen home-made soup)
2 cans salmon
1 can whole kernel corn
Lemon juice
Black pepper
Pasta
⅔ cup (50 g) grated cheese

Salted potato chips, broken up in the bag (if you have a very large bag, use the equivalent of 2 or 3 small packages)

1. If necessary, thin the soup with a little milk or tomato juice—or a combination of the two—and if you're using another homemade soup from the freezer, the same applies. (Defrost frozen soup first, preferably overnight at room temperature, or in the microwave.)
2. Drain the cans of salmon and corn and empty into a large ovenproof dish. Sprinkle with lemon juice and black pepper and mix in the tomato soup and uncooked pasta (approximately one very generous handful per person).
3. Scatter the grated cheese and crushed chips over the top and bake in a moderate oven, 350°F (180°C) for about 30–40 minutes.

## THURSDAY:
## PORK LOIN CHOPS, SAUSAGES & RICE WITH SALAD

1. Cook the sausages (Bratwursts again) in the oven preheated to 400°F (200°C). Season the pork, drizzle with a little olive oil, and put under a preheated broiler on the highest setting, turning at least once.
2. Wash the rice and put in a pan of slightly salted boiling water. Boil rapidly for a couple of minutes then cover with a lid and simmer very gently, checking after about 12 minutes to see if it's done.
3. Make salad with tomatoes, spinach, and cucumber from this week's shopping list, plus anything else you have and want to include.
4. Strain the rice in a colander, rinse well with boiling water, and serve everything together.

FRIDAY:
BREAD ROLL PIZZAS
Large soft bread rolls
Olive oil
Onions
Leftover bacon and/or sausage
Spinach
Mushrooms
Tomatoes
Tomato paste or ketchup
Pineapple
Grated cheese

1. Slice the bread rolls in half and lightly toast the underside of each half under the grill while you warm some oil in a large pan.
2. Finely chop whatever you have to use for the toppings and fry everything except the pineapple for a few minutes, enough to soften the onion and brown the meat a little. Add the pineapple to the mixture.
3. Spread the upper side of the bread rolls with tomato paste or ketchup, cover with the mixture, top with grated cheese, and place under a hot grill for a few minutes, until the cheese has melted, browned, and bubbled.

# WEEK FIVE

| | |
|---|---|
| MONDAY: | Corned Beef Haşh |
| TUESDAY: | Fish Stick Pie |
| WEDNESDAY: | Spaghetti Bolognese |
| THURSDAY: | Curried Nut Roast & Rice |
| FRIDAY: | Bacon, Egg & Homemade French Fries |

THE SHOPPING LIST:
- Ground beef (about 2 pounds)
- Corned beef
- Bacon joint (cured pork, ham)
- Fish sticks
- Eggs (6 free-range)
- Cheese
- Spaghetti
- Rice
- Bread
- Peanuts
- Tomato paste
- Whole kernel corn
- Stock cubes (×12)
- Baked beans
- Potatoes
- Spinach
- Mixed bell peppers
- Mushrooms
- Onions
- Carrots
- Asparagus
- Tomatoes
- Cucumber

# WEEK FIVE: THE RECIPES

MONDAY:
CORNED BEEF HASH WITH BAKED BEANS

Lots of potatoes (at least 2 large per person)
Oil
Corned beef
2 large onions

1. Peel and boil the potatoes until they're just done and then cut into cubes.
2. Warm the oil in a very large frying pan (or a large deep-sided pan to give you more room to maneuver) while you cut the corned beef into chunks and slice the onions.
3. Fry the onions and potatoes in the hot oil add and the corned beef once the onions are starting to brown.

4. Fry for a few more minutes until it looks good to you, and serve with baked beans or any fresh green vegetables, canned, or other frozen vegetables you might have.

TUESDAY:
FISH STICK PIE WITH POTATO WEDGES AND CORN OR FISH STICK PIE (page 106).

1 Preheat oven to 450°F (230°C). Give the potatoes a quick wash with a vegetable brush in a bowl of cold water; cut lengthwise into wedges, place on a large ovenproof tray, drizzle with oil and bake for 20–25 minutes.

2. Get the rest of the ingredients ready and cook the fish sticks according to the package directons about halfway through the potatoes' cooking time.

WEDNESDAY:
SPAGHETTI BOLOGNESE
Try breaking up the spaghetti into small pieces before putting into boiling water, or if you have small children who prefer pasta shapes, use them instead.

1 pound package (500g/1lb) ground beef
1 onion, finely chopped
Mushrooms, sliced
1 carrot, grated
2 cloves garlic, crushed
1 can chopped tomatoes (about 14.5 ounces/411 g)
Tomato paste
1 beef stock cube
Dried oregano or mixed Italian herbs

1. Cook the meat in a large pan over a medium heat (occasionally turning it over with a wooden spoon) while you prepare the vegetables.
2. Strain the meat to get rid of as much of the excess fat as you can. Add the finely chopped onion, mushrooms, grated carrot, crushed garlic, chopped tomatoes, tomato paste, stock cube, and seasoning, and cook for a few more minutes.
3. Adjust the consistency of the Bolognese sauce with more tomato paste to make a richer sauce, or add a little beef stock (or ½ glass of wine) if you want to thin it down.
4. Simmer gently for about 15 minutes while you cook the spaghetti. Serve with grated cheddar cheese or Parmesan.

THURSDAY:
## CURRIED NUT ROAST
This nut roast is delicious hot or cold with salad and rice, or on its own with chutney or a yogurt dressing. Buy peanuts in the shell if you can't get shelled peanuts in the supermarket, or try a local shop; you'll find large bags of shelled nuts in any good Asian food store. If you can only get salted peanuts though, taste the cooked nut roast before adding any extra salt at the table, or give the peanuts a rinse in cold water at Step 2 *(see page 86.)*

Fresh bread crumbs made with 4–5 slices of white bread
½ pound (225g) peanuts or cashew nuts
1 large onion
2 small bell peppers (red/orange and green)
2 cloves garlic, crushed
Olive oil
Sunflower/corn oil

1 can chopped tomatoes (about 14.5 ounces/411 g)
Marjoram or mixed herbs
3 teaspoons curry powder
1 teaspoon ground cumin
1 egg, beaten

1. Make the bread crumbs in a blender or food processor then put them in a very large mixing bowl.
2. Put the nuts into the food processor and process for about half a minute then add them to the bowl.
3. Meanwhile, chop the onion and peppers and fry with the crushed garlic in a mixture of olive oil and sunflower or corn oil, until the onion is crisp and golden.
4. Add the fried vegetables to the bowl with the chopped tomatoes, herbs, spices, and beaten egg and mix thoroughly (use a fork, it's easier) to bind everything together.
5. Press the mixture into a well-greased, standard-sized loaf pan (long-strip-lined with wax or parchment paper) and bake in the oven preheated to 400°F (200°C) for about half an hour, until golden.
6. Cook the rice and make salad while the nut roast is in the oven. Cut the nut roast into slices and serve.

FRIDAY:

BACON, EGG, AND HOMEMADE FRIES
There's no fry like a homemade fry and they're dead easy to make yourself, although you wouldn't think so to hear some celebrity chefs' advice on the subject. In an article I read not long ago some of them had very complicated instructions, which included rinsing the potatoes under cold running water for 5 minutes (5 minutes! Doesn't anyone have a water meter?), flash-frying in hot oil, then

sprinkling them with this and that before finally finishing them off in the oven.

All you really need is good potatoes (Maris Pipers are ideal) and a very large saucepan about two-thirds full of hot oil—unless you've got an electric fryer (I haven't) in which case you'll know what to do.

Roast or boil the bacon joint the night before if you don't have enough time the same evening, then carve it into thick slices to be re-heated (covered in a casserole dish) in the microwave. Alternatively, buy ham steaks, which just need to be broiled about halfway through the fries' cooking time.

1 bacon joint (or 4–6 gammon [ham] steaks)
Potatoes
Oil
6 eggs
Asparagus
Salt and pepper

1. Peel the potatoes, cut into fries roughly ½ inch (2cm) thick and rinse well in cold running water for a mere 30 seconds.
2. Allow the potatoes to drain while you heat the oil, making sure you've got rid of every last drop of water by blotting with an old, clean tea towel or paper towels.
3. When a cube of stale bread dropped into the oil turns golden within seconds, the oil is hot enough.
4. If you have a frying basket large enough, use that, otherwise cook the fries loose, lowering them into the hot oil as carefully as you can.
5. Cover with a lid and check them often; they should be ready in about 20 minutes.

6. Remove the fries from the pan with a slotted spoon and drain them on plenty of paper towels on a large baking sheet while you quickly fry an egg for each ham steak and cook the asparagus spears in the microwave, according to the instructions on the package.

# Index

Alcohol, 14
  Beef Stroganoff, 64–65
  Celery Soup, 113–14
  Ginger Beer, 215–17
  Medallions of Lamb in Red Wine, 67
  using stout for stock, 64
All-in-One Apple Cake, 182
Allspice, how to use, 12
Almond & Apricot Muffins, 187–88
Aluminum foil, using, 76
Apple Cider, Cider Sauce for Sausages, 57–58
Apple Pie
  Poor Man's Apple Pie, 142
  using apple pie mix, 12
Apples
  All-in-One Apple Cake, 182
  Baked Apples, 139–40
  Sweet Apple & Apricot Pork, 61
  Toffee Apples, 217–18
Applesauce, using store-bought, 59
Apricot
  Almond & Apricot Muffins, 187–88
  Sweet Apple & Apricot Pork, 61
Artichokes, how to prepare, 12–13
Asparagus, how to prepare, 13
Avocado Sandwiches, 22

Bacon
  Bacon, Egg & Homemade Fries, 253–55
  Bacon Cakes, 103–4
  Boiled Bacon & Roast Potatoes with Roasted
    Vegetables, 241–43
  Hash Browns, Bacon & Beans, 24
  The Healthiest English Fry up Possible, 25
  Liver, Bacon & Onions, 246–47
  Noodles, 101–2
  Spicy Bean Soup, 118–19
Bad eating habits, 8–9
Baked Apples, 139–40
Baked Banana Custard, 152
Baked Potato Pizza, 90–91
Bananas
  Banana Cake, 181
  Banana-Orange Trifle, 142–43
  for breakfast, 19
Beans
  Bubble, Bangers & Beans, 238–39
  Chili Con Carne, 43–45
  Corned Beef Hash with Baked Beans,
    250–51

Hash Browns, Bacon & Beans, 24
The Healthiest English Fry up Possible,
  25
Spicy Bean Soup, 118–19
*See also specific types*
Beef
  Beef & Cheese Crumble, 47
  Beef Curry, 65
  Beef Stroganoff, 64–65
  Borsht, 123–24
  Chili Con Carne, 43–45
  Corned Beef Hash with Baked Beans,
    250–51
  cutting up with scissors, 64
  Frankfurters & DIY Pasta Sauce, 235
  Hamburgers, 45
  Instant Corned Beef Hash, 104–5
  Rissoles, 46–47
  Scotch Broth, 126–28
  stock, stirring mustard in, 64
Beets
  Borscht, 123–24
  how to prepare, 13
Beverages
  carbonated drinks, 8–9
  Ginger Beer, 215–17
  smoothies, 20, 156–57
Blanc, Raymond, 202
Boiled Bacon & Roast Potatoes with Roasted
  Vegetables, 241–43
Borscht, 123–24
Bran Loaf, 177–78
Bread
  Bread & Butter Pudding, 143–44
  Bread Pudding, 183
  Bread Roll Pizzas, 249
  Garlic Bread, 206–7
  Quick Brown Bread, 203–4
  Soda Bread, 204–6
  Things on Toast, 109
Breakfast, 17
  everyday breakfasts, 18–23
  weekend breakfasts, 24–25
Breakfast (everyday), 18–23
  avocado sandwiches, 22
  cake, 20
  cereal, 18–19
  eggs, 20–21
  fruit, 19–20
  pancakes, 22–23

Breakfast (weekend), 24–25
  Eggs Florentine, 24
  Hash Browns, Bacon & Beans, 24
  The Healthiest English Fry up Possible, 25
Broiled Sardines, 76
Brown Rice
  Kedgeree, 73–75
Bubble, Bangers & Beans, 238–39
Buns
  Hot Cross Buns, 211–14
Burgers
  Hamburgers, 45
  Veggie Burgers, 79–80
Butter
  Bread & Butter Pudding, 143–44
Butternut Squash
  how to prepare, 13
  Orange Squash Soup, 112–13

Cabbage
  Roast Chicken with Roast Potatoes and
    Parsnips, White Cabbage, Carrots, and
    Peas, 236–37
Cakes
  Bacon Cakes, 103–4
  for breakfast, 20
  Chocolate Rice Krispies Cakes, 168–69
  Cornflake Cakes, 169
  Cupcakes, 169
  Fastest-Ever Fishcakes, 108
  Fish Cakes, 75–76
Cakes (baking), 159–64
  approximate weights and measures,
    162–63
  best results, 163
  measuring, 162
  pans, 160
  pans, getting cake out, 161
  pans, lining, 160–61
  pans, putting cake in, 161
  telling when cake is finished, 161
  tips, 163–64
  what you need, 159–60
Cakes (special)
  Caterpillar Cake, 193–94
  Chocolate Caramel Cakes, 199–201
  Chocolate Jelly Roll, 193
  Chocolate Yule Log, 194–95
  Honey, Lemon & Yogurt Cake, 196–97
  Jelly Roll, 190–93
  Layer Cake, 195–96
  The Ultimate Chocolate Cake, 197–99
Cakes (wholesome)
  All-in-One Apple Cake, 182
  Almond & Apricot Muffins, 187–88

Banana Cake, 181
Bran Loaf, 177–78
Bread Pudding, 183
Carrot Cake, 176–77
Flapjacks, 183–84
Ginger Cake, 179–81
Muesli Muffins, 188–89
Plum Cake, 186–87
Pumpkin Muffins, 189–90
Rock Cookies, 178–79
Seed Cake, 184–86
Caramel
  Chocolate Caramel Cakes, 199–201
Carrots
  Carrot Cake, 176–77
  how to prepare, 13–14
  Roast Chicken with Roast Potatoes and
    Parsnips, White Cabbage, Carrots, and
    Peas, 236–37
Casserole
  Chicken & Leek Casserole, 237–38
Caterpillar Cake, 193–94
Cayenne Pepper, how to use, 12
Cebrian, Katherine, 154
Celeriac (celery root), how to prepare, 14
Celery Soup, 113–14
Cereal, 18–19
  Chocolate Rice Krispies Cakes,
    168–69
  Cornflake Cakes, 169
  Kellogg's All-Bran, 18
  muesli, 19
  oatmeal, 18
  shredded wheat, 18
  Weetabix, 19
Cheese
  Beef & Cheese Crumble, 47
  Cheese & Onion Tomatoes, 91–92
  Cheese & Spinach Omelette, 239–40
  Cheese & Zucchini Scones, 166–67
  Cheese Sauce, 81–82
  Cheshire Tart, 138–39
  Easy Cheesy Shortbreads, 165–66
  Eggs Florentine, 24
  Stuffed Mushrooms, 78–79
  *See also specific types*
Cheesecake
  Cherry Cheesecake, 135–37
  Cheshire Tart, 138–39
  Lemon Cheesecake, 137–38
Cherry Cheesecake, 135–37
Cheshire Tart, 138–39
Chicken, 47–48
  Chicken & Ham Pasta Bake, 52–53
  Chicken & Leek Casserole, 237–38

Chicken (*continued*)
  Chicken Curry, 50–51
  Chicken in Cream & Mushroom Sauce, 55
  Chicken Nuggets, 48–50
  Chicken Soup, 124–26
  Chinese Chicken Stir-Fry, 235
  Mexican Chicken, 51–52
  Roast Chicken with Roast Potatoes and
    Parsnips, White Cabbage, Carrots, and
    Peas, 236–37
  snacks, 155
  Sweet & Sour Chicken, 54
Children, 27–27
  alcohol and, 14
  and cake, 20
  and cereal, 18–19
  and fruit, 19–20
  fussy eaters, 28–32
  packed lunches, 32–37
Children (cooking with), 164–65
  Cheese & Zucchini Scones, 166–67
  Chocolate Chip Cookies, 175
  Chocolate Rice Krispies Cakes, 168–69
  Cornflake Cakes, 169
  Cupcakes, 169
  Cupcakes, Frosting, 169–70
  Easy Cheesy Shortbreads, 165–66
  Gingerbread Men, 171–72
  Jam Tarts, 167–68
  Sweetloaf, 172–74
  Treacle Crunches, 174
Chili
  Chili & Chips, 234
  Chili Con Carne, 43–45
Chilled Soups
  Cool Cucumber Soup, 128–29
  Hot or Cold Leek & Potato Soup, 129–30
Chinese Chicken Stir-Fry, 235
Chocolate
  Chocolate Caramel Cakes, 199–201
  Chocolate Chip Cookies, 175
  Chocolate Jelly Roll, 193
  Chocolate Marble Fudge, 226
  Chocolate Mousse, 146–47
  Chocolate Rice Krispies Cakes, 168–69
  Chocolate Yule Log, 194–95
  Coffee & Vanilla Fudge, 226
  Fudge, 224–26
  The Ultimate Chocolate Cake, 197–99
Chowder
  Smoked Mackerel Chowder, 122–23
Chutney, 218–19
  bottling, 218
Cider Sauce for Sausages, 57–58
Cinnamon, how to use, 12

Citrus fruit
  for breakfast, 19
  *See also specific types*
Coleslaw, 155
Cookies
  Chocolate Chip Cookies, 175
  Flapjacks, 183–84
  Gingerbread Men, 171–72
  Rock Cookies, 178–79
Cool Cucumber Soup, 128–29
Coriander, how to use, 11
Corned Beef
  Corned Beef Hash with Baked Beans,
    250–51
  Instant Corned Beef Hash, 104–5
  Shepherd's Pie, 39
Cornflake Cakes, 169
Cream
  Beef Stroganoff, 64–65
  Chicken in Cream & Mushroom Sauce, 55
Crumble
  Beef & Cheese Crumble, 47
  Rhubarb Crumble, 141–42
Cucumber
  Cool Cucumber Soup, 128–29
Cumin
  Chicken Curry, 50–51
  how to use, 11
  Spicy Pork Meatballs, 62–63
Cupcakes, 169
Curry
  Beef Curry, 65
  Chicken Curry, 50–51
  Curried Nut Roast, 252–53
  how to use, 11
  Sausage in Curry Sauce, 58
  Spicy Pork Meatballs, 62–63
Custard
  Baked Banana Custard, 152

Desserts, 133
  Baked Apples, 139–40
  Banana-Orange Trifle, 142–43
  Bread & Butter Pudding, 143–44
  Cherry Cheesecake, 135–37
  Cheshire Tart, 138–39
  Chocolate Mousse, 146–47
  English Fruit Fool, 149–50
  Lemon Cheesecake, 137–38
  Pastry, 134–35
  Poor Man's Apple Pie, 142
  Raspberry Ice-Cream, 144–46
  Rhubarb Crumble, 141–42
  Spotted Dick, 150–51
  tips, 133–134

Tiramisu, 148–49
Treacle Tart, 147–48
*See also* Cakes; Pies
Desserts (recipes in brief)
Baked Banana Custard, 152
Fruit Jell-O, 152
Orange Cups, 151–52
Strawberry Meringues, 151
Dinner (main recipes)
Baked Potato Pizza, 90–91
Beef Stroganoff, 64–65
Cheese & Onion Tomatoes, 91–92
Chicken & Ham Pasta Bake, 52–53
Chicken Curry, 50–51
Chicken Liver Risotto, 68–69
Chicken Nuggets, 48–50
Chili Con Carne, 43–45
Eggplant Lasagne, 80–82
Fish Cakes, 75–76
Fish Pie, 76
Ginger Beer Pork, 61
Greek-Style Pork, 63–64
Hamburgers, 45
Kedgeree, 73–75
Lancashire Hot Pot, 65–66
Lentil Moussaka, 82–84
Medallions of Lamb in Red Wine, 67
Mexican Chicken, 51–52
Moussaka, 42–43
Nut-Free Nut Roast, 86–87
Pizza, 87–90
Pork in Plum Sauce, 63
Ratatouille, 95–96
Rice Salad, 84–85
Rissoles, 46–47
Sausage Rolls, 59–60
Shepherd's Pie, 40–41
Spicy Liver & Pork Meatballs, 70
Spicy Pork Meatballs, 62–63
Stuffed Mushrooms, 78–79
Stuffed Peppers, 77–78
Sweet & Sour Chicken, 54
Sweet & Spicy Shrimp, 72–73
Sweet Apple & Apricot Pork, 61
Toad in the Hole, 56–57
Tuna Lasagne, 71–72
Veggie Burgers, 79–80
Dinner (recipes in brief)
Beef & Cheese Crumble, 47
Beef Curry, 65
Broiled Sardines, 76
Chicken Goujons, 55
Chicken in Cream & Mushroom Sauce, 55
Fish Pie, 76
Greek-style Pork, 63–64

Jamie Oliver–Style Pan-Fried Sausages, 58
Kebabs, 66–67
Liver in Black Bean Sauce, 69
Medallions of Lamb in Red Wine, 67
Mixed Grill, 70
Pork in Plum Sauce, 63
Sausages in Curry Sauce, 58
Spicy Liver & Pork Meatballs, 70
DIY Pasta Sauce, 93–94

Easy Cheesy Shortbreads, 165–66
Eggplants
Eggplant Lasagne, 80–82
how to prepare, 13
Lentil Moussaka, 82–84
Moussaka, 42–43
Eggs, 20–21
Bacon, Egg & Homemade Fries, 253–55
boiled, 21
Cheese & Spinach Omelette, 239–40
Eggs Florentine, 24
The Healthiest English Fry up Possible,
    25
Kedgeree, 73–75
open house eggs, 21
poached, 21
scrambled, 21
Shrimp & Egg Pie, 105–6
English Fruit Fool, 149–50

Fastest-Ever Fishcakes, 108
Fennel, how to prepare, 14
Fish and Shellfish, 70
Broiled Sardines, 76
Fish Cakes, 75–76
Fish Pie, 76
Fish Stick Pie, 106–7
Fish Stick Pie with Potato Wedges and Corn,
    106–7, 235, 251
Kedgeree, 73–75
Pacific Pie, 100–101
Salmon & Tomato Pasta Bake,
    247–48
Smoked Mackerel Chowder, 122–23
Sweet & Spicy Shrimp, 72–73
Tuna Lasagne, 71–72
*See also specific types*
Figgy Pudding, 221–24
Flapjacks, 183–84
Frankfurters
Frankfurters & DIY Pasta Sauce, 235
One-Step Pasta, 104
Fruit
for breakfast, 19–20
children and, 19–20

Fruit *(continued)*
English Fruit Fool, 149–50
Soft Fruit Spread, 219
*See also specific types*
Fruit Jell-O, 152
Fudge, 224–26
Chocolate Marble Fudge, 226
Coffee & Vanilla Fudge, 226

Garlic Bread, 206–7
Getting started, 5–7
Ginger
Ginger Beer, 215–17
Ginger Beer Pork, 61
Ginger Cake, 179–81
Gingerbread Men, 171–72
how to use, 11
Goat Cheese
Stuffed Mushrooms, 78–79
Grapefruit
for breakfast, 19–20
Grapefruit Curd, 210
Greek-Style Pork, 63–64
Grocery shopping (weekly menu planning)
week 1, 233
week 2, 236, 237
week 3, 241
week 4, 245–46
week 5, 250
Guacamole, 207
Gunther, John, 16

Ham
Chicken & Ham Pasta Bake, 52–53
Hamburgers, 45
Hash
Corned Beef Hash with Baked Beans, 250–51
Instant Corned Beef Hash, 104–5
Hash Browns, 210–11
Hash Browns, Bacon & Beans, 24
Healthiest English Fry up Possible, The, 25
Herbs & Spices, 10–12
mixed herbs, 12
Honey, Lemon & Yogurt Cake, 196–97
Honeycomb, 214–15
Hot Cross Buns, 211–14
Hot or Cold Leek & Potato Soup, 129–30
Hot Pot
Lancashire Hot Pot, 65–66
Hummus, 207–8

Ice-Cream
Raspberry Ice-Cream, 144–46
Instant Corned Beef Hash, 104–5
Isotonic Drinks, 157

Jam Tarts, 167–68
Jamie Oliver–Style Pan-Fried Sausages, 58
Jell-O
Fruit Jell-O, 152
Jelly Roll, 190–93
Johnson, Samuel, 158

Kebabs, 66–67
Kedgeree, 73–75
Kellogg's All-Bran, 18
Bran Loaf, 177–78
Kidney
Mixed Grill, 70
Kidney Beans
Chili Con Carne, 43–45

Lamb
Kebabs, 66–67
Lancashire Hot Pot, 65–66
Medallions of Lamb in Red Wine, 67
Moussaka, 42–43
Shepherd's Pie, 40–41
Lancashire Hot Pot, 65–66
Lasagne
Eggplant Lasagne, 80–82
Tuna Lasagne, 71–72
Layer Cake, 195–96
Lebowitz, Fran, 26
Leek
Chicken & Leek Casserole, 237–38
Hot or Cold Leek & Potato Soup, 129–30
Lemon
Lemon Cheesecake, 137–38
Honey, Lemon & Yogurt Cake, 196–97
Lentils
Lentil & Vegetable Soup, 117–18
Tomato & Red Lentil Soup, 119–20
Lentil Moussaka, 82–84
Liver, 67–68
Chicken Liver Risotto, 68–69
Liver, Bacon & Onions, 246–47
Liver in Black Bean Sauce, 69
Mixed Grill, 70
preparing, 68
Spicy Liver & Pork Meatballs, 70
Loaf
Bran Loaf, 177–78

Mackerel. *See* Smoked Mackerel
Mayonnaise, 209–10
Meat
ground meat, 39
*See* Beef; Kidney; Lamb; Liver; Pork
Meat Soups, 111
Borscht, 123–24

Chicken Soup, 124–26
Scotch Broth, 126–28
Meatballs
Meatballs, Tagliatelli & Tomato Sauce, 244
Spicy Pork Meatballs, 62–63
Medallions of Lamb in Red Wine, 67
Meringues
Strawberry Meringues, 151
Mexican Chicken, 51–52
Minestrone, 120–22
Mixed Grill, 70
More Noodles, 102–3
Moussaka
Lentil Moussaka, 82–84
Moussaka (with Lamb), 42–43
Mousse
Chocolate Mousse, 146–47
Muesli, 19
Muesli Muffins, 188–89
Muffins
Almond & Apricot Muffins, 187–88
Muesli Muffins, 188–89
Pumpkin Muffins, 189–90
Mushrooms
Beef Stroganoff, 64–65
Chicken in Cream & Mushroom Sauce, 55
Stuffed Mushrooms, 78–79

Noodles, 101–2
More Noodles, 102–3
Nut-Free Nut Roast, 86–87
Nutmeg, how to use, 12
Nuts
Almond & Apricot Muffins, 187–88
Curried Nut Roast, 252–53
Roasted Nuts, 208–9

Oatmeal, 18
Oliver, Jamie, 40, 148
Omelettes
Cheese & Spinach Omelette, 239–40
One-Step Pasta, 104
Onions
Cheese & Onion Tomatoes, 91–92
Liver, Bacon & Onions, 246–47
Oranges
Banana-Orange Trifle, 142–43
for breakfast, 19
Orange Cups, 151–52
Orange Squash Soup, 112–13
Orwell, George, 98

Pacific Pie, 100–101
Pancakes, 22–23
freezing, 23

Peanut Butter Pancakes, 23
variations, 23
Pantry (basic ingredients), 9–10
bottled goods, 10
can goods, 9
dried goods, 9–10
other, 10
Paprika, how to use, 12
Parmesan Cheese
Stuffed Mushrooms, 78–79
Parsley, how to use, 11
Parsnips
Roast Chicken with Roast Potatoes and
Parsnips, White Cabbage, Carrots, and
Peas, 236–37
Pasta
Chicken & Ham Pasta Bake, 52–53
Eggplant Lasagne, 80–82
More Noodles, 102–3
Noodles, 101–2
One-Step Pasta, 104
Salmon & Tomato Pasta Bake, 247–48
Spaghetti Bolognese, 251–52
Tuna Lasagne, 71–72
*See also specific types*
Pastry, 134–35
Peanut Butter Pancakes, 23
Peas
Roast Chicken with Roast Potatoes and
Parsnips, White Cabbage, Carrots, and
Peas, 236–37
Peppers
Stuffed Peppers, 77–78
Pies
Fish Pie, 76
Fish Stick Pie, 106–7
Fish Stick Pie with Potato Wedges and Corn,
106–7, 235, 251
Pacific Pie, 100–101
Poor Man's Apple Pie, 142
Shepherd's Pie, 40–41
Shrimp & Egg Pie, 105–6
Pizza, 87–89
Baked Potato Pizza, 90–91
Bread Roll Pizzas, 249
toppings, 89–90
Plums
Plum Cake, 186–87
Pork in Plum Sauce, 63
*See also* Prunes
Poor Man's Apple Pie, 142
Pork
Boiled Bacon & Roast Potatoes with Roasted
Vegetables, 241–43
Ginger Beer Pork, 61

Pork (*continued*)
Greek-Style Pork, 63–64
joint of pork, roasting, 59
Meatballs, Tagliatelli & Tomato Sauce, 244
Noodles, 101–2
Pork in Plum Sauce, 63
Pork Loin Steaks, Sausages & Rice with Salad, 248
Sausage Rolls, 59–60
Spicy Pork Meatballs, 62–63
Sweet Apple & Apricot Pork, 61
Potatoes
Bacon, Egg & Homemade Fries, 253–55
Boiled Bacon & Roast Potatoes with Roasted Vegetables, 241–43
Hash Browns, 210–11
Hash Browns, Bacon & Beans, 24
Hot or Cold Leek & Potato Soup, 129–30
Moussaka, 42–43
Potato Salad, 210
Potato Wedges, 235
Roast Chicken with Roast Potatoes and Parsnips, White Cabbage, Carrots, and Peas, 236–37
Shepherd's Pie, 40–41
Sweet Potato soup, 116–17
Prunes
for breakfast, 20
*See also* Plums
Pudding
Bread & Butter Pudding, 143–44
Bread Pudding, 183
Figgy Pudding, 221–24
Pumpkin
how to prepare, 14
Pumpkin Muffins, 189–90
Pumpkin pie mix, using, 12

Quantities, 15
Quick Brown Bread, 203–4
Quick Fixes, 99
Bacon Cakes, 103–4
Fastest-Ever Fishcakes, 108
Fish Stick Pie, 106–7
Instant Corned Beef Hash, 104–5
More Noodles, 102–3
Noodles, 101–2
One-Step Pasta, 104
Pacific Pie, 100–101
Shrimp & Egg Pie, 105–6
Smoked Salmon Tagliatelli, 107–8
Things on Toast, 109

Ramsay, Gordon, 148
Raspberry Ice-Cream, 144–46

Ratatouille, 95–96
Recipes
alcohol in, 14
quantities, 15
and salt, 15
servings, 15
Rhubarb Crumble, 141–42
Rice
Kedgeree, 73–75
Pork Loin Steaks, Sausages & Rice with Salad, 248
Rice Salad, 84–85
Rissoles, 46–47
Risotto
Chicken Liver Risotto, 68–69
Rissoles, 46–47
Roast Chicken with Roast Potatoes and Parsnips, White Cabbage, Carrots, and Peas, 236–37
Roasted Nuts, 208–9
Rock Cakes, 178–79
Rosemary, how to use, 12

Sage, how to use, 12
Salad
Potato Salad, 210
Rice Salad, 84–85
Salmon
Fastest-Ever Fishcakes, 108
Salmon & Tomato Pasta Bake, 247–48
Smoked Salmon Tagliatelli, 107–8
Salt, 15
Sandwiches
Avocado Sandwiches, 22
Hamburgers, 45
Veggie Burgers, 79–80
Sardines
Broiled Sardines, 76
Sauce
Cheese Sauce, 81–82
Cider Sauce for Sausages, 57–58
DIY Pasta Sauce, 93–94
Sausages, 55
Bubble, Bangers & Beans, 238–39
Cider Sauce for Sausages, 57–58
The Healthiest English Fry up Possible, 25
Jamie Oliver–Style Pan-Fried Sausage, 58
Mixed Grill, 70
More Noodles, 102–3
Pork Loin Steaks, Sausages & Rice with Salad, 248
Sausage in Curry Sauce, 58
Sausage Rolls, 59–60
Toad in the Hole, 56–57

Scones
   Cheese & Zucchini Scones, 166–67
Scotch Broth, 126–28
Seed Cake, 184–86
Servings, 15
Shepherd's Pie, 40–41
Shortbreads
   Easy Cheesy Shortbreads, 165–66
Shredded wheat, 18
Shrimp
   defrosting, 70
   Fish Pie, 76
   Shrimp & Egg Pie, 105–6
Sweet & Spicy Shrimp, 72–73
Smith, Sydney, 110
Smoked Mackerel
   Kedgeree, 73–75
   Smoked Mackerel Chowder, 122–23
Smoked Salmon Tagliatelli, 107–8
Smoothies, 156–57
   for breakfast, 20
Snacks, 155–56
Soda Bread, 204–6
Soft Fruit Spread, 219
Soup, 111
   Celery Soup, 113–14
   Lentil & Vegetable Soup, 117–18
   Minestrone, 120–22
   Orange Squash Soup, 112–13
   Smoked Mackerel Chowder, 122–23
   Spicy Bean Soup, 118–19
   Stinging Nettle Soup, 115–16
   Sweet Potato Soup, 116–17
   tips, 111–12
   Tomato & Red Lentil Soup, 119–20
   Watercress Soup, 114–15
   *See also* Chilled Soups; Meat Soups
Spaghetti Bolognese, 251–52
Spicy Bean Soup, 118–19
Spicy Liver & Pork Meatballs, 70
Spicy Pork Meatballs, 62–63
Spinach
   Cheese & Spinach Omelette, 239–40
   Eggs Florentine, 24
   Greek-Style Pork, 63–64
Spotted Dick, 150–51
Squash
   Orange Squash Soup, 112–13
Stinging Nettle Soup, 115–16
Stir-Fry
   Chinese Chicken Stir-Fry, 235
Stock
   stirring in mustard, 64
   using stout, 64
Strawberry Meringues, 151

Stuffed Mushrooms, 78–79
Stuffed Peppers, 77–78
Sweet & Sour Chicken, 54
Sweet & Spicy Shrimp, 72–73
Sweet Apple & Apricot Pork, 61
Sweet Potato Soup, 116–17
Sweetloaf, 172–74

Tagliatelli
   Meatballs, Tagliatelli & Tomato Sauce, 244
   Smoked Salmon Tagliatelli, 107–8
Tarragon, how to use, 12
Tarts
   Jam Tarts, 167–68
   Treacle Tart, 147–48
Things on Toast, 109
Tiramisu, 148–49
Toad in the Hole, 56–57
Toast
   Things on Toast, 109
Toffee Apples, 217–18
Tomatoes
   Cheese & Onion Tomatoes, 91–92
   Chili Con Carne, 43–45
   The Healthiest English Fry up Possible, 25
   Salmon & Tomato Pasta Bake, 247–48
   Tomato & Red Lentil Soup, 119–20
Tortilla
   Vegetable Tortilla, 243–44
Treacle Crunches, 174
Treacle Tart, 147–48
Trifle
   Banana-Orange Trifle, 142–43
Trillin, Calvin, 228
Tuna
   Fish Cakes, 75–76
   Fish Pie, 76
   Pacific Pie, 100–101
   Tuna Lasagne, 71–72
Twain, Mark, 38, 132

Ultimate Chocolate Cake, The, 197–99

Vegetables, 92
   Boiled Bacon & Roast Potatoes with Roasted Vegetables, 241–43
   Bubble, Bangers & Beans, 238–39
   DIY Pasta Sauce, 93–94
   Lentil & Vegetable Soup, 117–18
   preparing, 12–14
   Ratatouille, 95–96
   tips, 92–93
   Vegetable Tortilla, 243–44
   *See also specific types*

Vegetarian (mostly)
  Baked Potato Pizza, 90–91
  Cheese & Onion Tomatoes, 91–92
  Curried Nut Roast, 252–53
  Eggplant Lasagne, 80–82
  Lentil Moussaka, 82–84
  Nut-Free Nut Roast, 86–87
  Pizza, 87–90
  Rice Salad, 84–85
  Stuffed Mushrooms, 78–79
  Stuffed Peppers, 77–78
  Veggie Burgers, 79–80
  Veggie Burgers & Potato Wedges, 79–80,
    235

Watercress Soup, 114–15
Weekly Menu Planning, 229–31
Weekly Menu Planning (grocery shopping)
  week 1, 233
  week 2, 236, 237
  week 3, 241
  week 4, 245–46
  week 5, 250
Weekly Menu Planning (week 1), 231
  Chili & Chips, 234
  Chili Con Carne & Rice, 43–45
  Chinese Chicken Stir-Fry, 235
  Frankfurters & DIY Pasta Sauce, 235
  Veggie Burgers & Potato Wedges, 79–80, 235
Weekly Menu Planning (week 2), 232, 235–36
  Bubble, Bangers & Beans, 238–39
  Cheese & Spinach Omelette, 239–40
  Chicken & Leek Casserole, 237–38
  Kedgeree, 73–75
  Roast Chicken with Roast Potatoes and
    Parsnips, White Cabbage, Carrots, and
    Peas, 236–37

Weekly Menu Planning (week 3), 232, 240–41
  Boiled Bacon & Roast Potatoes with Roasted
    Vegetables, 241–43
  Meatballs, Tagliatelli & Tomato Sauce, 244
  Pacific Pie, 100–101
  Stuffed Peppers, 77–78
  Vegetable Tortilla, 243–44
Weekly Menu Planning (week 4), 232,
    245–46
  Bread Roll Pizzas, 249
  Liver, Bacon & Onions, 246–47
  Pork Loin Steaks, Sausages & Rice with Salad,
    248
  Salmon & Tomato Pasta Bake, 247–48
  Tomato & Red Lentil Soup, 119–20
Weekly Menu Planning (week 5), 232,
    249–50
  Bacon, Egg & Homemade Fries, 253–55
  Corned Beef Hash with Baked Beans, 250–51
  Curried Nut Roast, 252–53
  Fish Stick Pie with Potato Wedges and Corn,
    106–7, 235, 251
  Spaghetti Bolognese, 251–52
Weetabix, 19
Weight loss, 7–9
White Fish
  Fish Cakes, 75–76
  Fish Pie, 76

Yogurt
  as a basic, 10
  for breakfast, 19
  Honey, Lemon & Yogurt Cake, 196–97

Zucchini
  Cheese & Zucchini Scones, 166–67
  how to prepare, 14